Lifestyle Business Blueprint

Top 5 Strategies For Making Money Doing What You Love From Anywhere In The World

Tyler Basu
www.tylerbasu.com

Lifestyle Business Blueprint

Top 5 Strategies For Making Money Doing What You Love From Anywhere In The World

Copyright © 2015 by Tyler Basu

Published by Lifestyle Business Publishing

Cover Photo by Balazs Kardos

ISBN-13: 978-1508471646

ISBN-10: 1508471649

All rights reserved. This book and the information contained in it are proprietary in nature. No part of this publication may be reproduced, transmitted or sold without the prior written consent of the Author/Publisher.

No express or implied guarantees or warranties have been made or are made by the Author/Publisher regarding certain incomes, earnings, profits, and other financial claims. Individual results may vary, in large part, due to individual circumstances, activity, capability, as well as varying local and global market conditions and other factors. No responsibility or liability is assumed by the Author/Publisher for any injury, damage or financial loss sustained to persons or property from the use of this information, personal or otherwise, either directly or indirectly. While every effort has been made to ensure reliability and accuracy of the information within, all liability, negligence or otherwise, from any use, misuse or abuse of the operation of any methods, strategies, instructions or ideas contained in the material herein, is the sole responsibility of the reader.

All information is generalized, presented for informational purposes only, and presented "as is" without warranty or guarantee of any kind. This publication is designed to provide accurate and authoritative information in regard to the subject matter covered. It is sold with the understanding that the Author/Publisher is not engaged in rendering legal, accounting or other professional services. If legal advice or other professional assistance is required, the services of a competent professional person should be sought.

Any copyrights not held by the Author/Publisher are owned by their respective copyright holders. All trademarks and brands referred to in this book are for illustrative purposes only, are the property of their respective owners and not affiliated with this publication in any way. Any trademarks being used without permission and the publication of the trademark is not authorized by, associated with, or sponsored by the trademark owner.

Some of the links contained in this publication may be affiliate links and the Author/Publisher may be compensated for recommending those products or services. The Author/Publisher promises to never recommend any products or services that he has not personally used or does not believe in.

Praise for Lifestyle Business Blueprint

"The great thing about what Tyler does with this book is really make it about the audience. I've known and followed Tyler's career for a while and he truly lives by what he says. His tips about making money and building a lifestyle business are spot on as I myself have implemented these strategies. As we become more digitally connected it will become even more imperative to know how to launch successful businesses online and this is the book you need to read!" - **Tayo Rockson**, Entrepreneur & Host of the As Told By Nomads Podcast

"If you have dreamed of making money while you travel, then this is the book for you. There are several ways to become location independent, Tyler lays them all out for you along with case studies and examples. His writing style is easy to follow and addictive to read. Read this book, you will save yourself hundreds of hours and thousands of dollars." - **Matt Astifan**, Social Media Expert & Host of Internet Masterminds Meetup Group

"Well written business book on how to work and live and anywhere in the world while doing what you love." - **Gabriel Padva**, Principal Consultant at 30,000 FT Strategies

"My work involves helping baby boomers understand the concepts that Tyler presents in this book. It is so clean and simple that I have referred the book to some of my clients! I especially like the added value of the "Success Principles of Lifestyle Entrepreneurs" section. While having the strategies is great, the mindset is often overlooked and in my mind, equally important. Well done and highly recommended!"- **Charlie Poznek**, Business Coach & Host of The Boomer Business Owner Podcast

"Tyler is a great author and he knows his topics well. Thanks a million for the great advice and strategies in this book Tyler!" **- Joel Brown**, CEO & Founder of Addicted2Success.com

"Tyler provides a realistic look at lifestyle entrepreneurship, and gives actionable step-by-step plans to build your business. Where this book is at its best is in the case studies - real people like you and me who've escaped the corporate life." - **Nick Loper**, Founder of SideHustleNation.com

"This book is the quintessential guide to building a business that you can maximize your time and income without all of the costly mistakes. Tyler boils down each of his tried and tested strategies to only the simple steps you need to take to be successful. Don't waste your time with other books before getting all the key points here first. Tyler is a true lifestyle entrepreneur." **- Jason Francis**, Serial Entrepreneur

"Tyler has provided a solid framework for starting and growing an information product and coaching business online. Concise, direct, and to-the-point, this is not a book full of vague generalizations but specific, actionable information. Based on Tyler's own hands-on experience and insights collected from the several dozens of people he has interviewed, this book has all of the tools you need to get your business off the ground." – **Danny Flood**, Entrepreneur & Author of Buy Your Own Island

"As someone who was bitten by the "entrepreneur bug" a long, long time ago, I loved this book. Who doesn't want to work smarter - not harder - and reap the lifestyle to match? Lifestyle Business Blueprint has some great insights and is an easy read. Many of the tips/tricks contained within can be applied to anyone in business for themselves." – **Dai Manuel**, Fitness Blogger

Table of Contents

PREFACE 9
INTRODUCTION TO LIFESTYLE ENTREPRENEURSHIP 15
    Are You An Entrepreneur? 15
    A Lifestyle Entrepreneur Defined 16
    Characteristics of a Lifestyle Entrepreneur 17
    Finding Your Sweet Spot 19
TOP 5 STRATEGIES FOR MAKING MONEY DOING WHAT YOU LOVE 22
    STRATEGY #1: BLOGGING 24
        Introduction to Blogging 24
        Benefits of Blogging 25
        How to Make Money From Your Blog 27
        Steps for Getting Started 36
    STRATEGY #2: PODCASTING 49
        Introduction to Podcasting 49
        Benefits of Podcasting 50
        How to Make Money From Your Podcast 52
        Steps for Getting Started 59
    STRATEGY #3: INFORMATION MARKETING 72
        Introduction to Information Marketing 72
        Benefits of Information Marketing 73
        Getting Started With Information Marketing 79
    STRATEGY #4: FREELANCING 96

Introduction to Freelancing 96

Benefits of Freelancing 97

Getting Started As A Freelancer 102

How To Get Your First Client 107

STRATEGY #5: COACHING & CONSULTING 112

Introduction to Coaching & Consulting 112

Benefits of Coaching & Consulting 113

Getting Started as a Coach or Consultant....................................... 120

How To Get Your First Client 125

SUCCESS PRINCIPLES OF LIFESTYLE ENTREPRENEURS 132

PRINCIPLE #1: Think Like An Entrepreneur..................................... 134

PRINCIPLE #2: Serve A Hungry Market 137

PRINCIPLE #3: Your List = Leverage 140

PRINCIPLE #4: Congruency 146

PRINCIPLE #5: Focus On Income Generating Activities..................... 149

PRINCIPLE #6: Automation & Outsourcing 153

PRINCIPLE #7: What Gets Measured Gets Improved......................... 160

PUTTING IT ALL TOGETHER 163

PREFACE

September, 2015

I had no idea that one small decision would change the direction of my life entirely, but it did. It happened back in 2012, and I can remember the exact moment like it happened yesterday. I was sitting in a hotel conference room with about 1,000 other people, taking vigorous notes as the keynote speaker shared his wisdom about success and financial freedom.

I was 22 years old at the time, newly married, flat broke, with no idea what direction my life was heading in. Now I know you're probably thinking that those aren't uncommon circumstances for most 22 years-olds to be in (except for the married part, perhaps), but here's the thing: I wasn't your typical 22 year-old.

By that point I had already spent several years chasing financial success. I read a book called *Rich Dad Poor Dad* shortly after graduating from high school, and since then I became determined to become an entrepreneur and achieve financial independence. I seized every opportunity that came my way. I sold life insurance. I joined network marketing companies. I promoted seminars. I traded currencies. Let's just say I was willing to try anything.

At the age of 20 I moved across the country to help open a direct sales office, and I spent the next 18 months building sales teams and knocking on doors 6 days per week before finally admitting to myself that running a direct sales office was not going to be as easy or as enjoyable as I had hoped it would be. So as I sat in that seminar, I had already tasted my fair share of failed attempts to succeed. To say I was frustrated would have been an understatement. That's when it hit me...

There were people who achieved success in every one of the industries I had worked in. I just wasn't one of them. The industries weren't the problem - I was. Every one of those industries was just a vehicle. It's up to the person driving the vehicle to decide where they take it.

I realized that I needed to stop looking for the right vehicle to achieve success. What I needed to do was become the *right person*. If I became the right person, it wouldn't matter which vehicle I used. *A good driver can use any vehicle to get where they want to go.* I'm just now reminded of a popular quote:

> "It's not enough to be in the right place at the right time. You have to be the right person in the right place at the right time." – T. Harv Eker

I decided to shift my focus from searching for strategies to achieve success, to learning the fundamental habits and principles that enable someone to succeed, regardless of which industry they're in or which strategy they use. *That shift in focus changed everything.*

I came up with an idea. My idea was to interview successful people from different industries in order to find the common threads between them. There was just one problem: I barely knew any successful people and I had no way to incentivize them to agree to an interview.

I decided that the next step for me to take would be to start a blog. I assumed that if I could set up a blog and build some sort of an audience online, then at least I would have a *platform* from which to reach out to successful people and ask for an interview. I was in the middle of taking a real estate course when I came up with the idea, so I waited a couple of months until I had a break from classes to get started.

A few months later, in June 2012, I launched www.ChattingWith Champions.com, and started conducting interviews. I published them directly on the website, and used social media to share the links to the interviews. I had absolutely no previous internet marketing experience (or interviewing experience, for that matter), so there was definitely a steep learning curve. But as I published more interviews, I started to build an audience. And as my audience grew in size, it became easier to attract more successful entrepreneurs to interview.

By the end of 2013 I had published over 30 interviews, written a few dozen articles, and attracted thousands of followers across various social media platforms. That's when I decided to launch the *Chatting With Champions Podcast*. I have since interviewed over 100 successful entrepreneurs, and my podcast has been downloaded by tens of thousands of people from all over the world.

As I've learned the habits and principles that have enabled the individuals I've interviewed to succeed, I've also implemented many of the same strategies that they've used to build their businesses. I've self-published several Amazon bestselling books (not counting this one). I've monetized my websites by including affiliate links in the recommended resources. I've coached other entrepreneurs and aspiring entrepreneurs, helping them to start blogs, publish books, launch podcasts, and position themselves as authorities in their industry. I also hired a virtual assistant who now works for me full-time, enabling me to focus my time on the activities that have the biggest impact on my business.

What's really cool is that I managed to make all of this happen from the comfort of my home using nothing but my laptop and a microphone. More importantly, I've learned to build a business doing something that I love. And to be honest, I still feel like this is just the beginning. This journey has allowed me to build relationships with individuals who are much more successful than I am, and seeing what they have been able to accomplish keeps me inspired to achieve so much more.

After several years of working part-time on my business, I decided it was time to take the leap. In the summer of 2015, I quit working in real estate in order to devote myself entirely to my digital publishing business. I hired more help, and after a few months of work we launched *Lifestyle Business Magazine*, a digital magazine for lifestyle entrepreneurs, which at this moment in time is my primary focus.

But this book isn't about me. In fact, this is the last time you will hear anything about me or my journey as an entrepreneur. **This book is about you.** It's about showing you how you can to turn your passions into a profitable business that you can run from virtually anywhere in the world, affording you a lifestyle that most people can only dream of.

I've divided this book into two main sections. In the first section I will be providing you with a detailed overview of 5 different strategies that you can use to build your own lifestyle business. In the second section I will outline 7 specific principles that lifestyle entrepreneurs adopt and that enable their long term success.

Throughout this book I will also be introducing you to many of the entrepreneurs that I have had the pleasure of interviewing. Their stories will serve as examples of how other people have used the strategies outlined in this book to build a lucrative business and live an awesome lifestyle.

Learning these concepts has absolutely changed my life and opened my eyes to a type of entrepreneurship that I never knew existed: *lifestyle entrepreneurship*. I am super excited to share these concepts with you.

Whenever you're ready, I'll meet you on the next page and we'll get started.

INTRODUCTION TO LIFESTYLE ENTREPRENEURSHIP

Are You An Entrepreneur?

The dictionary defines an entrepreneur as someone who organizes and manages any enterprise, especially a business, usually with considerable initiative and risk. This is a somewhat vague definition, but it's the definition we have all learned to accept. What it basically tells us is that if we have the initiative to start a business, and we're willing to risk failure in order to succeed, we are an entrepreneur.

Whoever is in charge of adding new terms to the dictionary doesn't seem to have figured out that there is a new type of entrepreneur that exists today. This new type of entrepreneur leverages technology, specifically the internet, to build a unique type of business. This entrepreneur uses a business as a means to provide valuable solutions to the marketplace, while simultaneously rewarding him with an enjoyable and fulfilling lifestyle. This entrepreneur designs his business to allow him to do the things he has a passion for, and to reward him with an abundance of time *and* money. This entrepreneur is known as a *lifestyle entrepreneur*.

A Lifestyle Entrepreneur Defined

Even though the term *lifestyle entrepreneur* is used and recognized by thousands of people around the world, there is no telling how much longer it will be before it finds its place in the dictionary. But when it finally does, its definition might look a little something like this:

> *A lifestyle entrepreneur is a business owner who prioritizes lifestyle benefits over profits. They organize and manage enterprises that can be fully or semi-automated, and are known for organizing their work and business activities around their lifestyle goals. Lifestyle entrepreneurs leverage other people and systems to run their business, are location-independent, and often work from home or while travelling.*

Characteristics of a Lifestyle Entrepreneur

To help you determine whether or not lifestyle entrepreneurship is for you, let us examine a few characteristics of a lifestyle entrepreneur:

1. They are location-independent

Unlike a traditional "brick and mortar" business owner, a lifestyle entrepreneur's business is not tied to any specific physical location. Their business exists *online*, and is therefore operational and accessible 24 hours per day, 7 days per week, 365 days per year. The internet never closes. They can work on their business from anywhere in the world as long as they have an internet connection. Even when they're not actively working on their business, it continues to run without them.

2. They leverage other people and technology to run their business

Lifestyle entrepreneurs design their business so that it literally *requires* them to do the things they are best suited for and most passionate about. All of the activities that are necessary to run a business but that they are not suited for or passionate about are handled by someone else or by a system. Unlike individuals who believe that *"if you want something done right, you have to do it yourself"*, lifestyle entrepreneurs are happy to utilize the talents of other people, and leverage systems and technology to run their business.

The goal of a lifestyle entrepreneur is to provide value to as many people as possible as efficiently as possible. They define efficiency as the wise use of available resources including time, money, and human capital. They are strong advocates of *outsourcing* and *automation*. They design their business to consume as few resources as possible while still remaining profitable. They create and manage efficient *systems*, enabling them to work *on* their business instead of *in* it.

3. They build a business that accommodates their lifestyle

Many entrepreneurs build a business at the expense of their lifestyle. They sacrifice precious time with their family, their health, travel or leisure, strictly for the pursuit of financial gain. This is not the case for a lifestyle entrepreneur.

A lifestyle entrepreneur's number one priority is *freedom*. Freedom to do what they want, when they want, where they want, and with whom they want. With freedom as their ultimate goal, they build a business that affords them the opportunity to spend time on areas of their life that are separate from their business.

A lifestyle entrepreneur defines success as being able to spend time on all of the areas of their life that are important to them: health, relationships, spirituality, personal development, philanthropy, recreation, travel, and so on. The accumulation of financial wealth is certainly one of their objectives, but it is not necessarily their primary objective. They view financial independence as something to be achieved so that they can focus their time and energy on things that are more important to them than money.

Finding Your Sweet Spot

Before we dive into some specific strategies that you can use to build a lifestyle business, let us not ignore a crucial business principle that must be adhered to if you are to succeed. For all intents and purposes, let's call it the principle of *finding your sweet spot*.

Each of the 5 strategies that you will be introduced to in this book have one thing in common: they all enable you to earn an income doing something that you are *passionate* about. However, you must not make the mistake of thinking that all of your passions are marketable or profitable. This is why you need to find your sweet spot.

What Is Your Sweet Spot?

Your sweet spot is the place where your passions intersect with your strengths and the needs of the marketplace.

Passion + Strength + Market Demand

= Sweet Spot

If you've ever watched one of those singing competition reality shows then you know that there are people who are passionate about singing but who are terrible at it. They are unlikely to succeed. Then there are people who are passionate about something, and good at it, but no one is willing to pay them for it. There is no demand for what they offer.

The harsh reality is that if there is no market demand for your product or service, it doesn't matter how passionate you are about it or how good you are at creating it, no one will buy it. There needs to be an obvious demand for whatever you're offering.

Finding your sweet spot will help prevent you from investing time, energy, and money building a business that provides something that no one really wants or needs. At the end of the day, people will only give you their money if you give them something in return that they value more than the money they exchange for it. If you aren't able to provide real value, or provide a solution to a real problem or challenge that someone is facing, the odds of your business succeeding are slim.

TOP 5 STRATEGIES FOR MAKING MONEY DOING WHAT YOU LOVE

In this first section of the book I'm going to introduce you to 5 specific strategies that you can use to make money doing something that you are passionate about. On their own, each of these strategies can be quite lucrative, but they also complement each other very well. Most of the case studies in this book feature entrepreneurs who have used several, even all of the strategies discussed in this book to build their business.

Keep in mind that these entrepreneurs didn't start by tackling multiple strategies at the same time. They started their business with just one of them. Once they achieved success with their chosen strategy, and systematized and automated it as much as possible, they were able to incorporate a second strategy into their business, and then a third, and so on.

If you try to tackle every strategy at the same time you will likely experience overwhelm and frustration. Start with one. Commit to it until you make it work. After you've achieved a fair amount of success with your chosen strategy, consider implementing another one. Success breeds success.

STRATEGY #1: BLOGGING

Introduction to Blogging

A blog is a website that is created with the purpose of informing and/or entertaining its visitors by providing them with free content to consume on a regular basis. That content is most often published in written format (referred to as articles or blog posts), although video blogs are also becoming more common.

There are many different types of blogs ranging from personal blogs, corporate blogs, expert blogs, and niche blogs. Each of these types of blogs serves a unique purpose and attracts a specific type of audience. Some blogs are considered more of a personal journal of their owner. Some are used to help increase awareness of an existing business's products or services. Some are used to help position their owner as an authority or expert in their industry.

The amount of visitors a blog attracts depends on a variety of factors including the quality of the content provided, how often new content is published, and the topics the blog focuses on. Common topics include technology, motivation, business, politics, current events, health, fitness, relationships, personal finance, spirituality, and so on. Some blogs attract hundreds of visitors per month, some attract thousands, and some attract as many as several million.

Benefits of Blogging

Regardless of which type of blog you decide to start, here are some of the benefits of having a blog:

1. Build your personal brand

Blogging is a great way to build your personal brand. When you publish valuable content about a specific topic on a regular basis, visitors of your blog begin to perceive you as an authority on that topic. Sharing your knowledge and expertise in written articles (or in video blogs), positions you as a thought-leader and expert in your industry. It also gives your readers a chance to get to know, like and trust you before they decide whether or not they want to do business with you.

2. Build and engage a community

A blog is a perfect platform to build and engage a community of individuals who share common interests. Don't think of your blog as a way to broadcast your content to the world, think of it as a place to initiate and facilitate conversations. Attract visitors to your blog by publishing great content, and then engage those visitors by encouraging them to share their feedback, questions, and opinions by commenting on your blog. When your blog's visitors are having conversations amongst each other in the comment section of your articles, you know you've built a community.

3. Create an asset that works for you 24/7

Every time you publish an article or a video on your blog, you create a digital asset that works for you 24/7. The internet never closes. You can be sleeping in your bed while someone halfway around the world is awake and enjoying your content. The value you provide to the marketplace is essentially multiplied by the number of posts you publish on your blog and how many people those posts reach.

4. Your content can go viral and attract new visitors

A blog post that is unique, informative, or entertaining will likely be shared by others. Every time someone decides to share your content, your blog gains exposure to new people. A single piece of content has the potential to reach thousands, even millions of people if everyone who finds it feels inclined to share it. This is how articles and videos go viral – through peer to peer sharing.

You can help your content to go viral by making it easy for it to be shared. Install social media plugins that enable visitors to share a blog post on a social media platform of their choosing with one simple click. The easier you make it for your visitors to share your content, the more it will spread.

How to Make Money From Your Blog

One of the most common questions aspiring bloggers ask is *can they make money from their blog?* The answer is yes, but as is true of everything, it will take some time before you reap the rewards of your efforts. That being said, here are a few of the ways you can make money from your blog:

1. Affiliate marketing

Affiliate marketing is a type of performance-based marketing that is conducted on the internet. Many companies create affiliate programs to enable other people to promote their products or services, and they pay those people a commission when their efforts result in a sale. When you sign up for a company's affiliate program, you are given a unique link to use when you direct people to that company's website or specific product/sales pages. They track the sales that come through your unique link so that they can pay you accordingly.

If you intend to recommend physical products, Amazon Affiliates is a great option. For digital products (ebooks, online courses, etc.), ClickBank is a great option. Both of these websites have thousands of products to choose from in virtually every category/industry you can think of.

Once you establish an affiliate relationship with a seller that offers products or services that would help your audience, you can monetize your blog by recommending those products or services to them. Here are three ways you can implement affiliate marketing on your blog:

Resource Page:

A resource page is a page on your blog that lists all of the various products and services that you believe are of value to your blog's visitors. For example, if the topic of your blog is health and nutrition, your resource page can contain a list of recommended products such as fitness equipment, vitamins, supplements, and so on.

Product Reviews:

Write an article or record a video that provides an extensive review of a specific product or service. To do this, you obviously have to purchase and use the product first. Share the benefits and the drawbacks, based on your experience with the product. Your reviews must be honest. A review is *not* a sales presentation.

Email Marketing:

Assuming you build an email list of people who subscribe to your blog, you can send your subscribers an email with a product or service recommendation in it. Don't go overboard with this strategy and start sending people offers as soon as they subscribe to your newsletter or they will probably unsubscribe (or worse, report your emails as spam). Earn the trust of your subscribers by sending them valuable information for free for an extended period of time. Once that trust is established, they will be more receptive to a product or service recommendation. Email marketing will be discussed in more detail in a later chapter.

2. Sell your own products or services

If you have your own products or services to sell, your blog is the perfect place to showcase them. This works very well for entrepreneurs who are using their blogs to position themselves as experts in their industry or niche. If you have a book, for example, you can use your blog to provide potential customers with valuable information about your area of expertise. If they want to learn about that topic in more detail, you can refer them to your book.

To promote your products or services from your blog, simply add a Product Page to your blog and list all of your products or services on that page. You can also place custom banner ads on your blog that link to sales pages for a specific product or service that you offer.

3. Advertising

For high traffic blogs (blogs that attract thousands of visitors or more on a daily basis), advertising is a viable option. With this model, you reserve space on your blog exclusively for advertisers to place their banner ads. When one of your visitors clicks on a banner ad, they are directed to that advertiser's website, and that advertiser pays you for sending that visitor to their website.

Generally speaking, this works best for high traffic blogs and is not a good strategy for a blog that attracts a small number of visitors per day. When someone clicks on an ad they are immediately re-directed to a different website, possibly never to return to your blog again. If your blog only gets a few visitors per day, the last thing you want to do is re-direct those visitors to another website. You want your visitors to stay on your blog as long as possible, and share your content with others so you get more visitors.

It is better to wait until your blog is attracting thousands of visitors per day or more before you place advertising on it. By that point there is more incentive for an advertiser to place an ad on your blog because they know it will exposed to a large audience. Think of a billboard on the side of a highway.

The cost to display an ad on that billboard will depend on how many cars drive by that billboard every day. The more exposure the billboard receives, the higher the cost to advertise on it. You can't expect to charge advertisers very much to place their ad on your billboard if very few cars drive by it every day. Plus, if your blog is attracting thousands of visitors per day it isn't as important to keep every single one of them on your blog for as long as possible. You can afford to let a few of them click on ads and leave your blog.

Here are two ways you can add advertising to your blog:

Google AdSense:

Google AdSense is a program run by Google that allows publishers to display different types of ads (text, image, video, etc.) on their websites that are customized based on the website's content. Basically, Google scans your blog for specific keywords, and then displays ads that are related to those keywords. For example, if you publish an article about real estate investing, the ads that appear on that page will most likely be real estate related.

The amount of money you earn when someone clicks on an ad depends on how much the advertiser is willing to spend to have their ad displayed. Some advertisers are willing to pay more than others, depending on what they're advertising and how much competition there is for the keywords they are targeting.

An attractive benefit of participating in Google's AdSense program is that it is very hands-off. Once you sign up for the program, you are given a unique ad code to paste into specific places on your blog (the header or sidebar, for example), and Google takes care of everything else. However, one drawback is that you have absolutely no control over what ads are displayed on your website, so there is a chance your visitors will be exposed to an ad that you would rather not have them exposed to. That being said, Google has algorithms to determine which ads your blog's visitors are most receptive to. To sign up for Google's AdSense program, visit www.google.com/adsense.

Sell advertising space:

If you want more control over the ads that are displayed on your blog, you can sell advertising space directly to advertisers. This process involves a lot more work on your part because you have to reach out to potential advertisers and negotiate a rate to charge them, but it can be quite lucrative if you know your audience will be particularly receptive to an ad for a specific product or service or from a specific seller.

If your blog is still relatively new, it is best to contact an ad broker to help you with this. In exchange for a fee, they will connect you with advertisers who would want to get in front of your audience. If your blog grows in popularity to the point where advertisers are contacting you directly, it is probably time to stop using an ad broker and deal with those advertisers directly.

CASE STUDY: RICKY SHETTY

After graduating from university with a degree in Psychology, Ricky Shetty decided to spend several years travelling the world. When he returned to his hometown of Vancouver, Canada in 2008, he got a job teaching English to ESL (English as a Second Language) students. He married his wife in 2011 and by 2012 they gave birth to their first child.

Wanting to be a good father, Ricky started searching the internet for parenting advice, but he couldn't seem to find very many good resources with parenting advice specifically for fathers. That's when he saw an opportunity to become that resource. He registered the domain www.DaddyBlogger.com and starting blogging regularly about his experiences as a father.

As Ricky blogged about fatherhood, he also began interviewing other fathers, asking them to share their advice on the subject. Ricky interviewed over 100 fathers from around the world. Shortly after, he decided to write a book to share the collective wisdom of all the fathers he interviewed. He self-published his book *Wisdom from Daddies* on Amazon, releasing it globally on Father's Day in 2013. He promoted the book to his blog's audience and network of fathers, and almost immediately, the book became a bestseller in its category.

Ricky's blog also includes reviews of family-friendly products and services, restaurant reviews, car reviews, family travel recommendations, contents, and giveaways. He monetizes his blog by utilizing affiliate marketing, writing sponsored posts, selling advertising space, and selling his own products and services.

Since launching *Daddy Blogger*, Ricky has become a recognized authority on fatherhood, social media marketing, and blogging. He has taught hundreds of other people how to start and grow a successful blog through live workshops and through his online course *Blog Mastery Workshop*. He is also the producer of the *Social Media Mastery Conference*.

To listen to my interview with Ricky visit:
www.chattingwithchampions.com/035

Steps for Getting Started

1. Choose a topic for your blog

The first step to starting a blog is to pick a topic to focus on. Choose a topic that you know a lot about and are passionate about, or that you are willing to learn a lot about over time. It is a good idea to search for existing blogs about the topics you are considering so that you can emulate what you like most about them, and also to start thinking about how you will differentiate your blog from theirs.

To search for existing blogs about your favorite topics, type those topics into a search engine along with the keyword *blog*. For example, if you are passionate about swimming, type "swimming blog" into Google and see which blogs appear in the search results.

2. Register a domain name and purchase web hosting

Once you've decided on a topic for your blog you'll need to come up with a name for it. It is best to choose a name that is memorable and that helps articulate the type of content that will be published on the blog. Some of the names of highly successful blogs include *TechCrunch*, *Mashable*, *The Huffington Post*, *ZenHabits* and *Elite Daily*. You can also come up with a tagline for your blog to help clarify its focus and positioning. For example, *Elite Daily's* tagline is *"The Voice Of Generation-Y"*.

If you intend to use your blog to build your personal brand it is wise to purchase a domain that contains your full name. For example, if your name is John Smith, you should register the domain www.johnsmith.com. If someone else already owns that domain, try searching for variations of your name such as www.john-smith.com or www.johnsmithblog.com. You definitely want a .com subdomain (instead of a .net or .org, for example). For video blogs, it is appropriate to use a .tv subdomain.

To check to see if your desired domain name is available, you can do a quick domain search using BlueHost. Once you register the domain name you want, purchase a hosting plan that includes WordPress. WordPress is the system you will use to set up your website and publish your blog posts.

3. Install a custom WordPress theme for your blog

A great place to search for WordPress themes is ThemeForest. They have thousands of themes to choose from, categorized by the types of websites they are intended for (news blogs, corporate blogs, personal blogs, etc.). Make sure the theme you purchase is responsive, which means that it can adapt to fit different screen sizes. If your theme isn't responsive, people will have a difficult time navigating your blog from smaller devices such as iPads or mobile phones, and they will likely leave out of frustration. Most responsive themes will cost less than $50.

Once you find a theme that you like and that you are confident will appeal to your blog's target audience, purchase the theme. Don't spend too much time trying to find the perfect theme when you're just getting started. If you want to install a different theme (or hire a designer to create a custom theme for you) at some point in the future, it is easy enough to do that. To install a theme on your blog, follow these steps:

- *Download your new theme as a zip file*
- *Login to your WordPress account*
- *On the left menu, click on Appearance, then click on Themes*
- *At the top of the page, click on Install New Theme*
- *Select the zip file of the theme you want to install*
- *Upload the theme, then click on Activate Theme*

4. Create the pages and menus for your blog

With your WordPress theme installed, the next step is to create the pages for your website. Your blog is technically just one section of your website (the section that contains the blog posts). At a minimum, you should create the following pages:

Home Page

This is the page people land on when they first visit your website. Most WordPress themes will allow you to customize the look of this page to suit your preference. Your home page should definitely display a list of your most recent blog posts.

About Page

This is the page that explains what your blog is about and who it is intended to serve. For personal blogs, it is appropriate to include your own biography on this page. Otherwise, a mission statement or clearly defined purpose for the blog will do.

Blog Page

This is the page that displays all of your blog posts in chronological order. You can also create pages that display blog posts from a specific category.

Contact Page

Provide your contact details on this page, or create a contact form for people to fill out if they want to get in touch with you.

Set up your main menu:

Once you've created these pages you will then want to add those pages to your website's main menu. Most menus are displayed in a bar across the top of the website, although you can also display menus on the sidebar or along the bottom of your website.

As you publish more blog posts, you should organize those blog posts into separate categories. Add each category to your menu so that visitors can easily navigate to blog posts related to a specific topic.

To create your menu, login to your WordPress dashboard and follow these steps:

- *On the left menu, click on Appearance*
- *In the sub menu, click on Menu*
- *Select a menu to edit (main menu, sub menu, or bottom menu)*
- *Select the pages and/or blog categories to add to the menu*
- *Click on Save Menu*

5. Install additional WordPress plugins

A newly created WordPress blog is designed to be lean and lightweight. Think of it as a stock model of a new vehicle that has not yet been equipped with any bells and whistles. To extend and add to the functionality of your blog, you'll need to install certain plugins. Plugins offer custom functions and features so you can tailor your website to your specific needs.

There are thousands of plugins available (some are free and some cost money), enabling you to do virtually anything you can think of to your website. To install a plugin on your blog, follow these steps:

- *Download the plugin as a zip file*
- *Login to your WordPress account*
- *On the left menu, click on Plugins, then click on Add New*
- *At the top of the page, click on Upload Plugin*
- *Select the zip file of the plugin you want to install*
- *Upload the plugin, then click on Activate Plugin*

Here are a few of the plugins you should install immediately to improve the functionality of your blog:

Akismet
This plugin filters comment spam so that it doesn't appear on your blog.

Google Analytics
In conjunction with your Google Analytics account, this plugin tracks important website statistics including the

number of visitors, page views, traffic sources, bounce rates, etc.

Pretty Link
This plugin allows you to create shorter links to specific pages on your blog.

WP Backup
This plugin backs up your blog on a regular basis in case you ever have to restore it to an earlier date.

Google XML Sitemaps
This plugin helps makes it easier for search engines to index your blog.

WordPress SEO
This plugin helps you optimize your posts for better rankings in the search engines.

Social Share Button
Your theme may already come with social media sharing buttons (to encourage your readers to share your content), but if it doesn't, this is a great plugin for that.

6. Publish your first posts

The process of publishing a post is pretty straight forward. On the left menu of your WordPress dashboard, click on *Posts* and then click on *Add New*. The basic elements of a post include its title, the main content (called the body), and an image. If you aren't able to finish writing a post in one sitting, you can save it as a draft. Once a post is complete and you're ready to publish it on your blog, click on *Publish*. You can also schedule it to be published at a specific date and time in the future.

What is most important is that your posts are actually enjoyed by your readers. Here are some guidelines to follow to ensure your posts are compelling and reader-friendly:

Write a captivating headline
This is probably the most important part of a post. If your headline doesn't grab someone's attention or arouse their curiosity, they probably won't even read your post.

Write like you talk
Use a conversational tone. Let your personality show in your writing. You don't want your readers to feel like they're reading a textbook or a college essay.

Use short paragraphs
Keep your paragraphs short (2-4 sentences). Long paragraphs can overwhelm the reader.

Tell a story
People can relate to a story more than they can relate to facts and figures. Stories are also much more memorable and enjoyable to read.

Use sub-headers or numbered lists

Break up your content into easily digestible sections using sub-headers or numbered lists. This helps keep the reader engaged all the way to the end of the post.

Be bold

Don't be afraid to have an opinion. Be willing to be controversial. Polarize your audience.

Include a call to action

Don't leave your reader wondering what they should do next. Give them something to do. Tell them how they can use the information they just learned, encourage them to comment, or ask them to subscribe to your newsletter.

7. Promote your posts

Every time you publish a new post, you should promote it to as many people as possible. Having a pre-determined strategy for promoting new content will help give your blog posts the initial boost they need to go viral.

Social media is a great place to share your posts. Consider setting up a profile for your blog on Facebook, Twitter, LinkedIn, Google Plus, and any other platforms that are appropriate considering your target audience. To simplify the sharing process, you can use a social media management tool such as HootSuite. This will allow you to share a link to your latest post on multiple social platforms at the same time, and even schedule specific posts to be shared at pre-determined times in the future.

8. Invite others to become guest contributors

Unless you're willing to pay other people to contribute content for your blog, when you first get started you should be prepared to be the only person creating content for it. It is difficult to persuade people to contribute content to your blog for free when it is brand new, because they have no guarantee that the content they create for you will be seen by enough people to make it worth their time to do so.

Once you get some traction with your blog and you've built up an audience, you can leverage that audience to attract guest contributors. These contributors provide you with content for free in exchange for the exposure that they will get from having their content published for your audience.

To encourage people to become guest contributors, make it obvious that you offer that opportunity. Include a link in the main menu or sidebar of your blog to a page that outlines the process by which someone can become a guest contributor. Provide them with specific guidelines to follow as they create content for your blog. This will ensure the content people submit to you requires very little revision or editing before you publish it.

CASE STUDY: JOEL BROWN

At the age of 24, Joel Brown was working as a Sales Executive for a telecommunications company in Perth, Australia. With only a few hundred dollars to his name, he was determined to change his circumstances and eventually own his own business. He attended seminars, took courses, and read books about entrepreneurship, personal development and success. Fuelled by his passion for those subjects, Joel decided to start a blog.

Joel registered the domain www.addicted2success.com and set up a blog with the intention of educating and inspiring like-minded people from all over the world. He started blogging regularly, resorting primarily to Twitter to share his articles and build an audience before branching into other social media platforms.

After nine months of blogging, Joel signed up for Google's AdSense program. This allowed members of Google's ad network to display their banner ads on his blog. The revenue he generated from the ads wasn't much at first, but he continued to work hard and publish new content regularly. As he produced more content, traffic to his blog increased along with the blog's number of followers on social media. Within two years he was making as much money from his blog as he was from his job. That's when he decided to quit his job to run his blog full time.

Today, *Addicted 2 Success* has numerous guest authors contributing their articles to the site, has hundreds of thousands of followers across multiple social media platforms, and attracts millions of readers on a monthly basis. Joel also wrote an ebook, *The Formula: The Secret Ingredients Of Online Success*, which he sells directly from his website. The combined revenue from his website and ebook sales is well over six-figures per year, enabling Joel to spend his time travelling the world and working with other entrepreneurs to help them achieve success.

To listen to my interview with Joel visit
www.chattingwithchampions.com/036

STRATEGY #2: PODCASTING

Introduction to Podcasting

Ever since Apple released its first iPod and literally revolutionized the way we consume audio content, podcasting has experienced a significant increase in popularity. The term *podcast* actually derives from a combination of the words *iPod* and *broadcast*. Its recent surge in popularity is likely caused by the sheer number of portable media devices available to us today, coupled with our desire to find and consume content that we are interested in.

A podcast is essentially a collection of digital media files which are produced in a series, similar to a TV or radio show. There are audio and video podcasts, although for the purpose of this book, we will focus strictly on audio podcasts. You access a podcast using what is called a *podcatcher* (software that you install on your computer, audio player, or mobile device). If you subscribe to a specific podcast, your podcatcher will periodically check to see if any new episodes have been published and automatically download them for you.

Podcasting is most popular among people who want the ability to choose the content they consume. Unlike TV and radio, which are produced for mass consumption, most podcasts are produced to provide content for a more narrow audience with very specific niche interests. According to Apple, there are now more than 250,000 unique podcasts in more than 100 languages, and in 2013 the iTunes store counted over 1 billion podcast subscriptions. At this point in time, there are multiple podcasts for virtually any topic you can think of. And the best part is you can listen to them for free!

Benefits of Podcasting

Here are some of the benefits of podcasting:

1. Audio content is convenient to consume

Compared to other types of content such as text or video, audio content is very convenient to consume. Reading an article or watching a video requires you to focus 100% of your attention on that content, which comes at the expense of doing other activities.

A major benefit of listening to a podcast is that you can do it while you are doing something else. You can multi-task. Most podcast listeners listen to their favorite shows while driving, jogging, cleaning their house, exercising at the gym, etc. Doing so doesn't distract them from their current activity, it enriches it. A podcast can also be listened to from virtually any device including smart phones, tablets, and laptops. Even car manufacturers are beginning to incorporate access to podcasts directly from a car's stereo system.

2. Potential to reach a large audience

Making your podcast available on platforms such as iTunes or Stitcher exposes your show to a global audience that you likely would not reach if you published your content directly on your website. Millions of people listen to podcasts on those platforms, and they find new shows to listen to by searching for specific topics within those platforms.

For example, if you host a podcast about copywriting, someone looking for a podcast about copywriting is likely to find your show in their search results. Depending on your show's ranking and the size of the market for your topic, your show could attract hundreds, thousands, or even tens of thousands of listeners or more. Some podcasts attract *millions* of listeners every month.

3. Position yourself as an authority in your industry

Hosting a podcast is a great way to position yourself as a thought leader and authority in your industry or niche. Much like having a blog or publishing a book, hosting a podcast helps build your reputation as an expert. It is a way for you to attract people who want to learn more about a specific topic, and become known as an expert on that topic. Many podcast hosts are able to attract lucrative opportunities including paid speaking engagements, book deals, sponsorships, and coaching or consulting clients thanks to their show.

4. Hearing your voice builds rapport and trust

When someone hears your voice, it is incredibly personal. They can hear your excitement and emotion. It can be difficult to convey those things with written words. When someone listens to your voice while exercising at the gym, or driving in their car for example, it can feel as if you are having a 1-on-1 conversation right there with them.

As people listen to more of your episodes, they will develop a familiarity with your specific communication style and tonality. Your style may even repel certain people, and that is perfectly fine. Your unique style is not meant to attract everyone. Over time, the people who come to know, like, and trust you will become your loyal listeners, and the ones who don't will move on to another show.

How to Make Money From Your Podcast

1. Affiliate marketing

If you recommend specific products or services on your show, a simple method for profiting from that recommendation is to establish an affiliate relationship with that product or service's seller.

For example, if you recommend a book on your show, you can sign up for the Amazon Affiliate Program and obtain a unique link to that book. Include the link to that book on a *Recommended Resource* page on your website, or on the page of the specific podcast episode it was mentioned on. At the end of each episode, remind your listeners to visit that page if they are interested in the book. If they purchase the book using the link on your website, Amazon will pay you a commission for that referral.

2. Sponsorships

If your show's download numbers are high enough (several thousand per episode), finding sponsors for your show is a viable option. A sponsor is a company that pays you to recommend their products or services to your audience. Obviously, the higher the number of downloads your show receives, the more money you will make from this strategy.

Research shows that podcast listeners don't mind when the host takes a moment to acknowledge a sponsor during an episode. Many listeners even look forward to it, interpreting it as a helpful recommendation from a friend rather than "commercial interruption." Just make sure that every company you enter into a sponsorship agreement with offers products or services that are relevant and helpful to your audience. If they're not, you could lose your audience's trust, causing your show's download numbers to decline.

There are a few different ways to charge sponsors, the two most common ones being CPM (*cost per thousand*) and CPA (*cost per acquisition*). Using the CPM model, you would charge your sponsor a set price per one thousand listens (downloads). Using the CPA model, you would charge your sponsor a set price for each customer they acquire as a result of their exposure on your show (they will give you a unique link to their website to track this).

The current industry standard for podcast sponsorships is to mention your show's sponsor at the beginning of your episode (the "pre-roll") and in the middle of your episode (the "mid-roll"). A pre-roll typically lasts about 15 seconds and commands $18 per 1,000 listens (CPM). A mid-roll lasts about 60 seconds and commands $25 per 1,000 listens (CPM). You can therefore have 2 separate sponsors for the same episode, or sell both spots to the same sponsor as a package deal.

Although it is possible to mention your sponsor at the end of an episode, most podcast hosts agree that this is the best time to give your listeners a more personalized call to action such as to visit your website, subscribe to your podcast, leave a review for your show, join your email newsletter.

A simple way to find potential sponsors for your podcast is to listen to other podcasts that serve the same audience or focus on a similar topic as yours. Pay attention to who their sponsors are. If you think that any of those sponsors would be a good fit for your podcast, then visit their website, find their contact information and reach out to them. Again, you will need high download numbers to make this work. Each potential sponsor will want to see your track record of download numbers before agreeing to sponsor your show.

3. Promote your own products or services

One of the most efficient ways to make money from your podcast is to promote your own products or services on your show. When you consistently provide value to someone for free, they eventually feel inclined to reciprocate in some way. A podcast is an effective way to attract potential customers who may eventually be ready and willing to buy your products or services, such as books, courses, continuity programs, masterminds, and coaching or consulting.

A life coach, for example, can launch a podcast and use her show to share valuable advice with a very specific target audience (ie. her ideal client). At the end of each episode, she can invite her listeners to visit her website and request a free coaching session with her. Let's say 1% of her listeners take her up on that offer. In this scenario, she would book one free coaching session with a potential client for every 100 listeners. Imagine if she increases her conversion rate, or attracts thousands of listeners to her podcast, or both! This simple strategy can dramatically grow her business.

CASE STUDY: ANDREW FEREBEE

In 2013, Andrew Ferebee was working as a store manager for a large retail chain in San Diego, California. He was fresh out of college, and had followed the path prescribed to him by society: go to school, work for a big company, work your way up the ladder, etc. There was just one problem: he was miserable.

With no plan in place, but a determination to build a successful online business, Andrew quit his job in May 2013. He registered the domain www.KnowledgeForMen.com and dove head-first into blogging. He worked day and night to create inspiring content to help others, and within 6 months he was able to grow his blog from 500 visitors a month to over 500,000 visitors. But after several months of writing articles, Andrew started to run out of ideas for new content. As a way to bring new content and fresh ideas to his website, he decided to start interviewing successful people.

In November that year, Andrew launched the *Knowledge For Men* podcast - a podcast dedicated to providing men with the practical tools and resources to make real, concrete changes in their lives. His podcast features a combination of interviews with successful men, and occasional episodes of Andrew sharing key insights and lessons he's learned in his life. He promoted the podcast to his network and blog readers, catapulting his show to the #1 spot on iTunes New and Noteworthy in 3 categories.

To date, Andrew's podcast has received over 1,000,000 downloads worldwide, and he's had the pleasure of interviewing some very high profile guests including T. Harv Eker, Robert Greene, Jordan Belfort, and Tony Hsieh, just to name a few. He's monetized his podcast with affiliate marketing, sponsorships, and by promoting his own products and services which now include a private mastermind group, 1-on-1 coaching, and several online courses.

Andrew runs his business from the beach in San Diego, and spends his time living a healthy and active lifestyle doing yoga, lifting weights, running, reading every book he can get his hands on, and traveling the world in search of his next adventure.

To listen to my interview with Andrew visit
www.chattingwithchampions.com/056

Steps for Getting Started

1. Choose a topic for your show

The first step you should take is to decide on a topic that will become the focus of your show. You don't have to be an expert on the topic you choose (you'll understand why in the next step), but you definitely need to have enough interest in your chosen topic to ensure your passion and enthusiasm for your show does not diminish over time.

Spend some time entering specific keywords into the search bar in iTunes (narrow your search results to podcasts only). Type in some of your favorite topics and see what comes up. You want to get a good idea for what podcasts about your chosen topic already exist so you can think of ways to differentiate your show from the existing ones.

2. Choose a show format

Once you've decided on a topic, the next step is to choose a format for your show. Here are the common formats for audio podcasts:

Self-hosted
You are the only host for your show. You have complete control.

Co-hosted

You co-host the show with a partner. It is important to choose a partner who compliments you and who can commit to co-hosting the show for a reasonable period of time.

Interviews

You host the show, but you interview a guest for each episode. This is a great option if you want to learn about a specific topic, and use your podcast as leverage to reach out to people you want to learn from.

Self-produced

You host the show and you provide the content for each episode. This is a great option if you are an expert (or want to position yourself as an expert) on a topic in which you have lots of knowledge and experience.

Consider which format is best for you in the long-run. Mixing it up sometimes is fine too. For example, there are many podcast hosts who stick mostly to the self-produced format, but occasionally interview a guest for one of their episodes.

3. Show name, website, and cover art

As you consider a name for your podcast, you should also be searching for available web domains. Ideally, you want a domain that matches the name of your podcast. For example, if you're thinking of calling your podcast "The Dog Lover Show" you should check to make sure that *TheDogLoverShow.com* is available, or alternatively, *TheDogLoverPodcast.com* or perhaps just *TheDogLover.com*.

BlueHost is a great place to do a domain search and purchase web hosting. If you already have a website, and a podcast will be an additional content creation strategy for your existing brand, you can skip this step.

The next step is to have your cover artwork created. If you're on a tight budget, you can use Fiverr and have a few different designs made for $5 each and then choose the best one. For a higher quality design, use 99Designs. Your cover art should be 1400 by 1400 pixels in size. This will be the image people see when they find your podcast online. It is important to have a cover art that appeals to your target audience and that is consistent with your brand.

4. Buy the necessary equipment and software

Fortunately, the equipment required to host a podcast has become very inexpensive. Less than a decade ago, you would have had to spend thousands of dollars on equipment in order produce a podcast with the same sound quality that can be produced for a few hundred dollars today. In addition to your computer or laptop, all you need to get started is a microphone, a pair of headphones, and some programs/software for recording and editing your episodes.

Here are some popular microphones used by podcast hosts today (listed in order from least expensive to most expensive):

Logitech ClearChat
Audio-Technica ATR2100
Blue Yeti
Heil PR-40

You should also consider purchasing a pop filter to go with your microphone. This will help reduce the "popping" sound caused by the push of air from your mouth as you speak.

Here is a list of the programs/software you will need:

For conducting calls (for co-hosted shows or interviews) use Skype

For recording your calls and saving them as MP3 files use MP3 Skype Recorder, Pamela (for PC), or Ecamm Call Recorder (for Mac)

For editing your audio files, and for recording a self-produced show use Audacity, GarageBand (for Mac), or Adobe Audition

5. Record your intros and outros

Every episode of your podcast should have an intro and outro. These help your show sound professional. Listen to a few of the intros and outros of other podcasts to get some ideas for what style you like best.

AudioJungle is a great place to purchase royalty-free music to use for your intro and outro. Once you find the music you like, write a script for your show's introduction. You can record your own voice, or hire someone to do it for you. Then you combine the two recordings so the voice and the music overlap. You can do the same thing for the outro. Once you've got the final versions complete, save them as MP3 files. You will refer back to these files each time you publish a new episode for your podcast.

6. Record your first episodes

With your intro and outro files ready, you can start recording your first episodes. Whether you record an interview with a guest or just your own voice, the process is the same. Open the file for the new recording along with your intro and outro files in whatever editing program you use. Then copy your new recording and paste it right in between the intro and the outro. You are essentially creating a new file that includes your show's intro, the specific episode, and the outro all together. Save it as an MP3, and name the file accordingly (for example: *"XYZ Podcast Episode 001"*).

Your first podcast episode should be an introduction to your show. Tell the listener who you are, why you created the show, what topics you will focus on, and what format and frequency they can expect going forward. This will allow people who discover your podcast for the first time to refer back to your first episode and immediately determine whether or not your show is something they will be interested in.

7. Tag your audio files

Podcast platforms function like a search engine. For example, if someone is looking for a podcast about real estate on iTunes, they will likely type "real estate" into the search bar. iTunes will then present them with a list of podcasts that are relevant to real estate.

Tagging an audio file is the process of adding information into that file (episode title, description, copyright information, artwork, etc.). Podcast platforms recognize the information in audio files, which helps them to rank your podcast in the search results for certain terms.

A simple way to tag an audio file is to create a playlist in iTunes on your computer. Each time you create a new episode, drag that file into the playlist. Then, right click on the file and click on "Get Info". From there, you will be able to manually add the appropriate information to the file. Once you've tagged a file, it is ready to be published.

8. Upload your audio files to a media host

Uploading your audio files directly to your website is not a good idea. If hundreds or even thousands of people are listening to an audio file that is stored on your website's server at the same time, it is going to slow down your website dramatically. You need to host your audio files on a separate server – a media host's server. This way, people can access your podcast episodes from your website (and from podcast platforms), but when they download and listen to the audio file, they are actually doing so from the media host's server and not your website's server.

The most popular media host for podcasts today is Libsyn. They have several hosting plans to choose from that range in price depending on how many audio files you intend to upload to their server each month and how big those files are. When you upload a file, you will be given a unique download link that you can copy and paste onto your website.

9. Submit your show to podcast directories

If you make it all the way to this step, congratulations! Setting up a podcast involves way more technical steps than most people are comfortable with. This is the last major technical step you have to go through. After this, there are minimal ongoing technical steps required to run your show.

Assuming your website runs on WordPress, you'll need to install a plugin called [Blubrry Power Press](#). There are some settings within this plugin that you will need to configure (such as adding your show name, description, cover art, etc.) but it is pretty straightforward. There are plenty of free video tutorials online to guide you through this process if you need additional help.

Once you've configured these settings correctly, this plugin will provide you with a unique URL (called a feed) for your podcast. This is the feed you will provide to podcast directories like iTunes and Stitcher in order to get your show listed on those platforms. Once your submission gets approved, your podcast will appear on those platforms. They will scan your website regularly for new podcast episodes using the feed you provided, and whenever they detect a new episode has been published, they will display it on their platform. Once this process is established, it is very hands-off.

When you're ready to publish a new podcast episode, create a new post in WordPress, just like you would if you were creating a blog post. With the Bluebrry Power Press plugin installed, you will see a place for you to paste the link to a specific podcast episode as you're creating your new post. This is the same link you obtain from your media host when you upload an audio file to their server. Paste the link, publish the post, and voila, your podcast episode will be online and ready to share.

10. Promote your show!

Once your podcast is live, it's time to tell the world! Share the links to your podcast episodes on social media. Send an email to your list of subscribers when you publish a new episode. Tell people you meet in person about your show. Ask your listeners to rate and review your podcast on iTunes, Stitcher, etc. This will help increase your show's ranking on those platforms.

If you host an interview show, ask your guests to share the link to their interview with their network. This will help to expose your show to new audiences. That being said, you should not *depend* on your guests to promote your show for you. Many of them do interviews regularly, and are not comfortable promoting every single one of them to their network. At the end of the day, promoting your show is your responsibility. It is *your* show.

CASE STUDY: JOHN LEE DUMAS

After graduating from Providence College, John Lee Dumas was commissioned as an Officer in the US Army. After a 13-month tour of duty in Iraq, followed by seven more years of service in the Unites States, John set out to find a 'normal' job as a civilian.

He gave Law School a try, but it wasn't for him. Instead, he moved to Boston and accepted a corporate job in finance. 18 months later he quit his job and moved to New York City where he worked for a tech start-up company, but he still hadn't quite found what he was looking for. He then moved to San Diego, California and started working in real estate.

Working in real estate meant that driving became a big part of John's daily routine. In need of something that could help him pass the time while driving, a friend of his suggested that he listen to podcasts. Almost immediately, John started listening to podcasts on a daily basis. He especially liked listening to interviews with successful entrepreneurs.

At the time, most podcasts were publishing new episodes on a weekly basis. As a daily podcast listener, John was listening to more content than any one show was creating. Consequently, John had to keep finding new shows to subscribe to. John realized that if he was experiencing this problem, other people must be too. That's when he came up with the idea to start his own podcast – a daily podcast.

In September of 2012, John officially launched *Entrepreneur On Fire*, a podcast where John interviews today's most successful and inspiring entrepreneurs, 7 days a week. Launching a daily podcast was not an easy task. John regularly worked over 12 hours per day to maintain his daily publishing schedule and build his audience. Fortunately, his hard work and dedication eventually paid off.

Entrepreneur On Fire was awarded Best Of iTunes 2013, and by the end of 2014 it was receiving over 1,000,000 downloads per month. John has interviewed over 800 entrepreneurs, been featured in both TIME and Inc. Magazine, and built a thriving community of loyal listeners that he lovingly refers to as *Fire Nation*.

Once he had enough listeners, John was able to monetize his show through sponsorships and affiliate marketing. He then created several free tutorials and online training programs to help others do the same, including his two signature programs: *Podcaster's Paradise* and *Webinar On Fire*. He is also the author of *Podcast Launch*, a book he published on Amazon. John's business now generates multiple six-figures per month in revenue, which he reports in detail every month on his website.

To listen to my interview with John visit
www.chattingwithchampions.com/060

STRATEGY #3: INFORMATION MARKETING

Introduction to Information Marketing

We live in what is often referred to as the *Information Age*. As you know, the internet provides us with access to ridiculous amounts of information, and more of it is created every single day. Finding the information we need on any given topic can be overwhelming. Most of us do not have the time to sift through all of the information that is out there or try to figure out which of it is credible, relevant, and applicable to our unique circumstances. This is precisely why people are willing to pay for specific information that is organized and delivered to them in a format they can readily and easily consume.

People are buying information on virtually every topic imaginable – from gardening, to dog training, to parenting, to dating, to fitness, and everything else in between. If you have specific knowledge on a certain topic, you have an incredible opportunity to organize and package that knowledge into a digital product that you can sell online. Information marketing is essentially the process of identifying a topic that people have an interest in, and then packaging and selling a product that teaches them about that topic or helps them solve a specific problem.

Benefits of Information Marketing

Information products exist in many forms and price ranges. There are traditional books, ebooks or PDFs, online courses, audio programs, video programs, DVD programs, newsletters, and webinars, just to name a few. Their prices can range from a few dollars to a several thousand dollars each. Regardless of which type of product you create or which price point you sell it at, here are some of the benefits of creating and selling an information product:

1. Multiply yourself (leverage)

With information marketing, you do the initial work to create a product one time, and then set up marketing systems to continue to sell that product after you created it. It takes a lot of work to create a product, but once it is created you can sell it many times, often for a period of several years. Essentially, you get paid over and over and over again for the work that you do *one time*.

Each time you create a product, you create an asset that continues to make money for you. Every product you create becomes an additional revenue stream to your business. The value you provide to the marketplace gets multiplied with each product you create and with each customer that purchases your product. This is called *leverage*.

2. Minimal interaction with customers

In many cases, you can sell an information product without ever meeting or communicating with your customer. This is accomplished by setting up systems (or leveraging existing systems) to process the sale and handle the fulfilment for you. For example, if you publish a book on Amazon, you are leveraging Amazon's system to sell your book for you. People from all over the world can find your book, purchase it and download it without you having to do anything. It all happens automatically because Amazon has the systems in place to facilitate the transaction.

This is just one example, but the point is that there is no limit to the number of products you can create or the number of people you can sell those products to. This can be accomplished with little to no direct interaction with your customers. You can be sleeping in your bed while someone on the other side of the world that you don't even know buys your product.

3. Inexpensive to get started

Most information products are relatively inexpensive to create. Generally speaking, the more types of media that are used in a product, the higher its production cost. Simple ebooks or PDF guides have incredibly low production costs. Products with other types of media such as audio and video will require additional equipment to create (cameras, microphones, editing software, etc.) and will therefore have a higher production cost.

Depending on the types of media used in your product, your production costs can range from almost nothing, up to several hundred or even several thousand dollars. That being said, the most important cost to consider when you create an information product is your *time*. Information products require a significant amount of time to create. Don't create a product unless you have a reasonable expectation of generating a return on investment from your time.

4. High net profit potential

One of the most attractive benefits of selling an information product online is the profit potential. Not counting marketing costs (which apply to any business or product type) there are virtually no costs associated with selling and delivering your product to customers. You could sell a digital product for several thousand dollars and in many cases keep 100% of the revenue from the sale, minus any applicable merchant processing or transaction fees.

This is a characteristic that is unique to digital products sold on the internet. Physical products have production, delivery and fulfilment costs associated with every single sale. When a customer purchases a digital product, they are immediately given access to the product, or given a link to download the product. You can sell the same product 1,000 times and you only have to pay to create it once.

CASE STUDY: PEJMAN GHADIMI

Pejman Ghadimi is no stranger to hard work. He moved to the United States with his mother at the age of 12, and at age 14 he got his first job working as a telemarketer. Although he only worked part-time, Pejman made more calls and more sales than his colleagues, often earning as much as $2,500 per week in commissions. By the time he graduated from high school, he had already been promoted to Director of the company.

At 18 years old, Pejman accepted a position as a manager trainee for the retail side of a bank. He worked for the bank for 7 years, working his way up to Senior Vice President with a salary of $250,000 per year. Then, at the age of 25, he learned the hard way that there is no job security in corporate America. And just like that, he was let go.

Fortunately, Pejman utilized his spare time while working for the bank to create additional streams of income. In fact, through making multiple investments in real estate, and starting a detailing company that specialized in luxury vehicles, Pejman had already achieved financial independence.

With financial success no longer a primary concern, Pejman decided to shift his focus to finding ways to help other people succeed. This led him to create *Secret Consulting*, a branding and digital marketing agency that offers coaching services to individuals and small businesses. He also started a blog in 2006 called *Secret Entourage* where he began sharing the key concepts he had learned from his experiences.

It took a few years for Pejman to develop a loyal audience with his blog, but it eventually established a reputation as one of the go-to places to learn about success and entrepreneurship. Once he built a thriving community, Pejman was able to monetize his blog by offering educational products and training to his audience. He's published multiple books which are sold from his website and through various online retailers. He also created *Secret Entourage Academy*, a private membership community that features exclusive training and video interviews with some of today's most successful entrepreneurs. Today, the *Secret Entourage* brand reaches millions of people and has become one of today's most accepted forms of entrepreneurial education.

To listen to my interview with Pejman visit
www.chattingwithchampions.com/024

Getting Started With Information Marketing

There are many ways you can get started with information marketing. However, for the sake of not overwhelming you with too much information (no pun intended), we will examine 2 specific strategies you can use to create and sell an information product: writing a book and creating a course.

Write a book

How to write your book:

1. Choose a topic for your book

There are 2 methods you can use to pick a topic for your book. The first is to consider your interests, experiences, and expertise and then write a book to share what you know. The second is to do some market research to find out what topics people are actively searching for information on. If you choose the second option, you can write the book yourself after doing a considerable amount of research on that topic, or you can hire someone to write the book for you (a ghostwriter).

2. Create the title and subtitle

The title of your book (combined with the cover design) will have a major impact your book's sales. A great book with a vague title probably won't sell very many copies. Your title needs to be compelling. It needs to clearly articulate the subject matter of the book, and the benefit to the reader (the *result* it will help them get). When a potential buyer reads your book title you want them to think: "this is exactly what I am looking for."

Here are some examples of highly successful non-fiction book titles:

"How to Win Friends and Influence People" (Dale Carnegie)

"The 7 Habits of Highly Effective People: Powerful Lessons in Personal Change" (Stephen R. Covey)

"Start with Why: How Great Leaders Inspire Everyone To Take Action" (Simon Sinek)

"MONEY Master The Game: 7 Simple Steps To Financial Freedom" (Tony Robbins)

3. Create an outline

An effective way to come up with an outline for your book is to make a list of the most common questions your target market has about the specific topic. It is best to actually speak with potential buyers of your book instead of assuming what they want to know. For example, if you collect 10 questions from people who are interested in a topic, the answers to each of those questions can form the basis for 10 chapters in your book. Add an introduction and a conclusion, and voila, you have an outline.

4. Write the book

Once you have your outline complete, it is time to start writing the content for the book. Again, you can write it yourself, or hire a ghost writer to do it for you after providing them with the outline. If you want the book to contain your own words, but writing is not something you are particularly good at, a third option is to record your voice as you share your thoughts for each chapter, and then have that recording transcribed.

5. Edit and format the book

This is a somewhat tedious process, but it is very important. Once all of the content for your book is ready, it needs to be edited and formatted before it can be published. You can do this yourself or hire someone to help you. The purpose of this step is to fix grammatical errors and ensure consistent font types and sizes for all headings, subheading, and paragraphs. Even if your book has great content, skipping this step will make your book seem very unprofessional and most likely frustrate the reader.

6. Get a cover designed

The final step is to get a cover designed. Unless you have considerable experience with graphic design, you probably shouldn't do this yourself. There are many websites including Fiverr and 99Designs that you can utilize to find a designer. Provide the designer with the title of your book, some background information on your target audience, and samples of other book covers that you like. This will help the designer create something that will be appealing to your target audience.

How to sell your book:

Once your book is complete, it is time to sell it. Here are two specific options to consider for selling your book, each with their own pros and cons:

Self-publish on Amazon

Amazon, the world's largest online book retailer revolutionized the publishing industry when they introduced their Kindle Direct Publishing (KDP) program several years ago. Now, aspiring authors can self-publish their books on Amazon and immediately start selling copies to customers all over the world.

The greatest benefit of self-publishing your book on Amazon is your potential exposure to the millions of existing book buyers that browse Amazon's bookstore. If someone is searching for a book about a specific topic and your book appears in the search results, there is a chance they will buy it.

To publish your book on Amazon, you will need to create a KDP account. Once your account is set up, you can simply upload your book file, along with your cover and some additional details including your book description, keywords, contributors, and pricing. Once approved, your book will appear in Kindle format (ebook format) on all of Amazon's websites worldwide. If you price your book between $2.99 and $9.99, Amazon will pay you a 70% royalty on each sale. If you price your book below or above that price point, they will pay you a 35% royalty.

One drawback to self-publishing on Amazon is the price point most self-published books are sold at. The majority of ebooks are priced between $0.99 and $4.99. Since Amazon book buyers have become accustomed to buying books in these price ranges, charging a higher price will discourage most buyers. You will therefore need to sell hundreds or even thousands of books on a monthly basis to generate significant revenue.

Sell from your website

If you already have an audience that you've built through blogging, podcasting, or social media, you might want to consider selling your book directly from your website. The advantage of this is that you can charge whatever you want for your book and keep 100% of the revenue, less any merchant processing or transaction fees.

To sell your book from your website, you will need to install a payment system to process the transaction. E-junkie is a great option for this. They provide shopping carts and buy now buttons that you can use to sell digital and physical products. Once you set up your account, provide them with a PDF version of your book. When someone buys your book, they will be given a link to download that PDF file.

You'll also need to create a sales page for your book. This page acts as the salesperson for your book, and will work 24/7 to convert potential buyers into customers. Here are some of the important details to include on your sales page:

- *Your book title*
- *A picture of the book cover*
- *A description of the book or bullet list of learning outcomes*
- *List of testimonials from other readers*

- *Book price, terms, and refund policy*
- *A Buy Now button*

One drawback to selling your book directly from your website is that your book sales will depend solely on *your* marketing efforts. If you can't get the right people to visit your sales page, you won't sell very many copies. That being said, if you sell your book at a higher price point compared to what you would sell it for on Amazon, you can generate *more* revenue from *less* customers.

Create a course

How to create your course:

1. Choose a topic for your course

The first step to creating a course is deciding what to teach. Consider the specific skills you have acquired from your personal and professional experiences, and which of those skills you would be comfortable teaching to others. You don't have to be an "expert" on a topic in order to teach it, you just need to know more about it than the person you are teaching. For example, if you know how to conduct a job interview, design a logo, or set up a blog, you can create a course to teach someone who doesn't know how to do those things.

You may want to spend some time browsing through the various categories of online courses that already exist to help get some ideas. Udemy, one of the largest marketplaces for online courses, is a great place to do this. If several courses have already been created on a topic you are thinking of teaching, don't worry - that is a good sign. That means there is a demand for courses on that topic. You could even take those courses before you create yours so you can determine how you will differentiate your course from what is already available.

2. Create the title and subtitle

Just like with a book, the title of your course needs to be compelling and clearly articulate what is taught in the course. Here are a few examples of strong course titles:

"How To Design A Logo: A Beginner's Course"

"The Ultimate Gmail Productivity System For Business"

"How To Become A Bestselling Author On Amazon Kindle"

3. Create an outline

A course outline is essentially a course curriculum. Organize the topic you are teaching into several sections. Each section should contain a few lessons, each with a focus on one core concept or idea. Dividing your course into sections makes it easier for the student to learn the information. Remember, your students are paying to be presented with information in an organized and sequential manner. Here is an example of a course outline:

Course Introduction
Course Objectives
Instructor Bio
Section 1 (Outline & Learning Objectives)
    Lesson 1
    Lesson 2
    Lesson 3
Section 2 (Outline & Learning Objectives)
    Lesson 1
    Lesson 2
    Lesson 3
Section 3 (Outline & Learning Objectives)
    Lesson 1
    Lesson 2
    Lesson 3
Conclusion

4. Choose a format

Once you have your course outline created, it is time to decide on a specific format for your course. Consider which format is most appropriate for the topic of your course, and what your budget for producing it is. Some formats require more equipment to create and therefore have a higher production cost, so you'll need to plan accordingly. Here are the common formats used to create online courses:

Audio only
Record your voice as you teach. This is just like creating an audio book. Depending on your course topic, this may not be the ideal format for your student. For example, it is hard to teach someone to design a logo without actually *showing* them how to do it.

Screen capture with audio
Use screen recording software to record your computer screen as you demonstrate a specific technical process or use a specific program (for example: designing a book cover or setting up a blog). Use a microphone to record your voice as you perform the task.

Slideshow presentation with audio
Use screen recording software to record your computer screen as you give a slideshow presentation. Use a microphone to record your voice as you present the slides.

Audio and video
Use a microphone and a video camera to record live footage of you teaching (for example: a live workshop or seminar)

5. Record and edit your course

This is the most time-consuming step in the entire process. Depending on the length and format for your course, recording it can take anywhere from a few dozen hours to several hundred hours, plus the additional time it takes to organize and edit all of the recordings.

If your course is audio only, you can create it using the same equipment and software that was recommended in the chapter on podcasting. To record your computer screen, you'll need to purchase screen recording software. Screencast-o-matic is a good option for this.

If you choose to record live audio and video, you may want to hire a video production and editing team to ensure your final product is as professional as possible. This will require a greater financial investment upfront, but will allow you to charge a premium price for your course once it is created.

6. Create a course image and/or promotion video

The final step before you are ready to sell your course is to create a course image and/or promotion video to use in your marketing. This is a very important step, and the higher the quality of the course image and promotion video, the higher the perceived value of your course. Unless you are skilled with graphic design and/or video production, you should hire a professional to help you. Potential students will judge the quality of your course by the quality of its packaging. Your course image and promotion video are core components of its packaging.

How to sell your course:

Once your course is created, it is time to sell it. Here are two specific options to consider for selling your course, each with their own pros and cons:

Course marketplaces

A course marketplace is a website that hosts the courses of various course creators and splits the revenue from the sales of those courses with their respective creators. It's a lot like self-publishing a book on Amazon. You provide the course, they provide the platform from which to sell your course, and they keep a percentage of the revenue from every sale in exchange for doing so.

If you don't have much experience with creating and marketing online courses, or an audience to promote it to, this is probably your best option. You get to upload your course for free, and expose it to hundreds, even thousands, of potential students who may never have found your course otherwise. Some of the most popular course marketplaces include [Udemy](), [Skillfeed](), [Skillshare](), and [Lynda]().

A drawback to selling your course in a marketplace is that your course won't always sell for full price (thereby reducing the amount of money you earn from a sale). Many course marketplaces will run promotions and discount courses, which trains their database of customers to never pay full price for a course. That being said, the people who buy your course at a discount are people who probably would have never bought your course anyway if it wasn't in a marketplace.

Self-hosted

If you want complete control of your course and do not want to share the revenue from your sales with anyone, you can choose to self-host your course. Self-hosting requires a lot more work upfront compared to selling your course in a course marketplace, but it can be more profitable in the long run.

When you self-host your course, you essentially upload your course to your own website, and then sell it as a downloadable product from your website. Just like with selling an ebook directly from your website, you can use E-junkie to process the transaction.

Another option is to create a membership website (or add a members only area to your existing website) that restricts access to your course to paying customers only.

With a membership website, customers are given a unique username and password, which they use to log in to the website to access the course. MemberMouse is just one of many WordPress plugins that allow you to set this up.

There are also some costs associated with self-hosting your course, including domain registration fees, web hosting fees, and merchant processing or transaction fees. Since marketing your course will be your responsibility, so you should allocate a budget for that as well. The amount of sales you get will therefore depend on your ability to attract people to your website and convert them into paying customers.

CASE STUDY: STEFAN PYLARINOS

At the age of 21, Stefan Pylarinos and two of his friends started a dating coaching business. By this point, Stefan had spent several years developing the skills and the confidence to approach women, and he was prepared to teach those skills to others.

In an effort to learn how to get more people to attend their seminars, Stefan began to study internet marketing. He learned about blogging, copywriting, search engine optimization, email marketing, pay-per-click advertising, and so on. He and his two friends did what they could to try to make the business work, but for a number of reasons, the business failed and they each moved on to something different.

In the process of learning internet marketing, Stefan became attracted to the concept of creating passive income online. He decided to put his newly acquired internet marketing skills to use by creating a few blogs about home remedies for various skin conditions. Within a few months, the blogs were ranking in search engines and getting a decent amount of traffic. That's when Stefan put together an ebook and sold it directly from one of his blogs. He repeated this process multiple times in various niches, creating more blogs and ebooks. By the time he was 24 years old, he was earning over $5,000 per month in passive income online.

Achieving financial independence at a young age afforded Stefan the freedom to spend his time trying to discover what he was truly passionate about. He set up his own blog and YouTube channel called *Project Life Mastery*, and started sharing advice and concepts to help others in all areas of life. He also started offering life and business coaching to other individuals.

In 2012, Stefan took notice of Amazon's Kindle Publishing platform. Intrigued by this new platform, he re-wrote several of his blog articles, organized them into ebooks, and published them on Amazon. Almost immediately, the books started making a few hundred dollars per month. He then published more ebooks (some that he wrote himself, and some that he outsourced) until his portfolio of ebooks was generating several thousand dollars in royalties per month.

Stefan has since taught thousands of other people how to successfully publish ebooks on Amazon Kindle with his signature online course *Kindle Money Mastery*. By 2014, Stefan's income reached tens of thousands of dollars per month in passive, recurring revenue. Furthermore, his *Project*

Life Mastery blog, YouTube channel, and podcast have become a source of inspiration for thousands of people around the world on a regular basis.

To listen to my interview with Stefan visit
www.chattingwithchampions.com/030

STRATEGY #4: FREELANCING

Introduction to Freelancing

If you have any specialized skills, freelancing is a great way to get paid to do work that you enjoy and are good at. As a freelancer, you don't work for one specific company or organization as their employee, you work on a contract basis for as many different individuals or organizations as you want. Freelancers are essentially self-employed and treated as independent contractors.

Freelancers can charge by the hour, by the day, or on a per project basis. How much they charge is determined by a variety of factors including their experience, skill level, industry, rates of competing freelancers, and the cost of living in their country of residence.

Traditionally, most freelancers have been writers. But over the last few years as technology has evolved, freelancing has become common practice in almost every industry. Here are just a few examples of services that are in popular demand for freelancers today: graphic design, video or audio editing, writing, transcribing, copywriting, web development, illustrating, translating, researching, photography, journalism, event planning, and mobile app development.

Benefits of Freelancing

Here are some of the benefits of working as a freelancer:

1. Freedom and flexibility

Most freelancing jobs do not require you to be physically present in order to complete them. This enables you to work from virtually anywhere in the world, as long as you are able to communicate with your clients and deliver your work to them. You can essentially work from anywhere as long as you have an internet connection – from home, in coffee shops, and even while travelling.

Most clients will not care when you work, just that you complete your work in the agreed upon time frame. This means you can work on whatever days of the week you want, at whatever times are most convenient for you. You are free to set your own schedule.

2. Set your own rates

As a freelancer, you have the benefit of deciding how much you charge for your services. Of course, you must be aware of your skill level and market rates for your services. You don't want to charge too little for your services, but at the same time you wouldn't want to overcharge a client and upset them by submitting mediocre work. Charging a fair rate for your specific skills and expertise, and meeting (if not exceeding) your clients' expectations is the best way to stay in demand as a freelancer.

Once you know what your time is realistically worth, you are free to decline work from clients unwilling to pay you what you demand for your time and expertise. You are also free to increase your rates in direct proportion to your skill level and experience. As a general rule, as your skill level, experience, and credibility increase, so will your rates.

3. Choose your clients and projects

Having the freedom to choose who you work for and on what projects is one of the greatest benefits of being a freelancer. Unlike a salaried employee of one specific company or organization, you do not have a boss telling you what to do on a daily basis. In fact, you have the freedom to choose your "bosses" on a per project basis.

If you don't think you will enjoy working for someone, you don't have to work for them. Contrarily, if you are confident you will enjoy working for someone, you are free to accept the job. Having the freedom to choose the size, scope, and type of projects you work on ensures you spend your time only on tasks that you agreed to completing, and presumably, that you will enjoy doing.

CASE STUDY: MATT ASTIFAN

From a very early age, Matt Astifan dreamed of working in the film industry. He attended film school immediately after graduating from high school, where he was advised that the best way to learn film would be to actually work in the industry. Following that advice, Matt dropped out of film school early to find work in the industry. He worked as a Props Assistant at first and then later as an Art Director for several different Indie films.

A few years into his career, a writer's strike occurred, leaving Matt and the entire film industry with little to no work. After several months of having no income, Matt was forced to look for opportunities in other industries. The real estate industry was booming at the time, and many of Matt's friends who had become real estate agents encouraged him to do the same.

Matt took the real estate licensing course, passed the exam, and became a real estate agent. 9 months and no sales later, he was flat broke, carrying over $20,000 in credit card debt. Following the advice of his manager, Matt began studying internet marketing, thinking that doing so would help him with his real estate career.

Matt soon discovered that he had more passion for internet marketing than he did for real estate, so instead of continuing to work as a real estate agent, he started looking for work in the internet marketing space. He got a job selling search engine optimization (SEO) and websites on a commission basis to small and medium sized businesses, and in his spare time he learned as much as he could about the subject. He read books, bought online courses, went to seminars, networking events, and so on.

In 2009, Matt positioned himself as a freelance consultant specializing in social media marketing for businesses. He earned a full-time income teaching entrepreneurs how to develop and implement social media marketing strategies for their businesses. Matt soon realized that the majority of business owners didn't want to manage social media on their own. In response to the increasing demand for social media management, he shifted his focus in 2012 from training business owners to training other people to become social media marketing consultants.

Matt's staple program, the *Social Media Director Certification Program*, has certified over 100 people as Social Media Directors, who in turn have helped hundreds of businesses profit from social media. He is also the organizer of the *Internet Masterminds Meetup Group*, the largest internet marketing Meetup in the world.

Today, Matt spends his time working with internet marketing experts developing and promoting new programs for his company *Web Friendly*, in addition to building an online community which features videos from the weekly *Internet Mastermind* meetings.

To listen to my interview with Matt visit
www.chattingwithchampions.com/053

Getting Started As A Freelancer

1. Identify your strongest skills

The first step to becoming a freelancer is to take inventory of your current skills. Make a list of all of the different skills you have, and group them into related categories. Consider your past or current work experience, education, hobbies, etc. What specific tasks are you able to do exceptionally well? What is easy for you to do but difficult for others? What skills are you already being paid for?

2. Assess the market demand for those skills

Once you've identified some specific skills that you have, and that more importantly, you would enjoy doing, it is time to assess the market demand for those skills. The purpose of this step is to establish some realistic expectations about how much you can charge for certain types of work and who your typical client will be.

Spend some time browsing job postings in specific categories on the popular freelance networks (Elance, Odesk, and Guru are great starting points). These will give you a good idea of what your prospective clients are looking for. You should also take a look at the profiles of other freelancers offering similar services as you. Pay attention to how many years of experience they have, the number and quality of the reviews /testimonials their clients have given them, what country they are in, how much they charge, etc.

3. Build your portfolio

It is difficult to attract clients without a portfolio of your previous work to show them. To get started on building your portfolio, reach out to a few people who you believe could use your services, and offer to work on a project for free (or at a discounted rate). Explain to them that you are establishing yourself as a freelancer and are putting together a portfolio so that you can show showcase your work to potential clients. It shouldn't be very hard to convince someone to let you do some work for them, especially if you're not charging them a fee and therefore removing any financial risk on their part. You should also ask them for a testimonial once your work is complete so you can include it on your website.

4. Set up your website

Every freelancer should have their own website. There are certainly freelancers who find work strictly by creating profiles on freelance networks (more on that in the next step), but in the long run, having a website that you own and control is the best strategy for success. Freelance networks come and go, but your website will remain online for as long as you care to keep it. Having your own website also helps position you as a professional - it gives you credibility.

If you don't know how to set up a website, refer to the steps outlined in the first chapter on blogging. The process is essentially the same, but instead of installing a theme that was designed for a blog, you'll want to find a theme that was designed for freelancers. These types of themes are designed to emphasize the website owner's portfolio of work, instead of their blog articles. ThemeForest is a great place to browse for WordPress themes.

At a minimum, your website should include the following pages:

About Page

This is the page that contains your biography. Share where you're from, how many years of experience you have, what your skills are, what type of clients you work with, and why you love doing what you do.

Portfolio

This is the page where you showcase some of the work you've done for past clients. For example, an illustrator will often have samples of illustrations they've drawn for other authors or publishers on this page. Showcasing your work helps prospective clients decide whether or not you are suited for the work they require.

Testimonials

In most cases, your clients will not have the privilege of meeting you in person. Hiring someone that you find online and that you've never met before can be a risk for some people. Having testimonials from real clients that you've worked with and that were happy with your services helps reduce that scepticism. It's called *social proof*, and it is very effective.

Rates

This page is optional. If you charge by the hour, you may want to display your hourly rate. If your services tend to be highly customized based on the size and scope of each project you work on, it may be wiser to instruct your website visitors to request a quote from you after providing you with some more details about their needs.

Contact Page

Your website definitely needs to have a contact page. If there is no way for a prospective client to contact you after visiting your website, you might as well not have a website. Consider displaying your contact information (email, phone number, or Skype ID) directly on your contact page. Alternatively, you can insert a Contact Form for them to fill out. Forward all contact form submissions directly to your email, so whenever someone fills out the form their message is sent straight to your inbox.

5. Join freelancing networks

A freelance network is basically an online marketplace that enables freelancers and employers to find each other. As someone who is looking for a freelancer, you can post a job on these networks and wait for freelancers to contact you. As a freelancer, you can set up a profile on these networks, bid for jobs, and receive inquiries from potential clients who find your profile.

Having a profile on these networks is also a great way to increase your exposure online and direct potential clients to your website. There are numerous freelance networks online today, and again, Elance, Odesk, and Guru are great starting points.

6. Start networking

Lastly, don't be afraid to get out there and start networking. Go to events in your industry and let people know what services you offer. Connect with people on social platforms such as Facebook or Twitter. Add your skills and a link to your website to your LinkedIn profile. Order some business cards with your name, area of expertise, and contact information on them. Even though it is possible to build a successful freelancing business using only the internet, it never hurts to get out there and connect with people face-to-face.

How To Get Your First Client

With your website set up, and your profiles created on various freelance networks, you may start to get a few inquiries from potential clients. When that happens, you simply respond with a proposal, as outlined in Step 2 below. Eventually (and ideally), the majority of your clients will come to you in the form of repeat business and referrals, but getting to that level takes time. When you're first getting started, it's best to be proactive and actually *look* for work instead of waiting for it to come to you.

Here are 3 specific steps you can take to get your first paid client:

1. Apply for a specific job

Most freelance networks organize job postings by category. Bookmark the categories that reflect your skills and areas of expertise so that you can easily refer to the latest job posts in those categories. Jobs can get taken quickly (sometimes in as little as a few hours), so you'll want to check the job board in your chosen categories often.

2. Submit a proposal

When you see a post for a job that you are suited for, you need to submit a proposal (sometimes called a *bid*). In most cases this proposal can be brief – no more than 1-2 pages in length. Always customize your proposal to the specific job posting/client. A proposal that is obviously a copied and pasted template rarely gets responded to.

Your proposal should include a description of the project, a schedule, and a quote for your services. Depending on the nature of the project, you should consider including samples of your previous work in your proposal.

3. Get an agreement in writing

Once a client has agreed to work with you, it is best to put that agreement in writing and have it signed by both parties. Similar to the proposal, the agreement should outline the scope of the project, deliverables and deadlines, and payment schedule. You can use PayPal to create an invoice, send it to your client, and accept payment. It is wise to collect partial payment upfront and the balance upon completion of the project.

CASE STUDY: NICK LOPER

Nick Loper got his first taste of entrepreneurship by running a residential painting business while he was in college. Around that same time, he read a book called *Rich Dad Poor Dad* by Robert Kiyosaki which sparked his interest in real estate investing. At the age of 21, he bought his first investment property with the profits from his painting business.

Before he graduated from college, Nick accepted a part-time marketing internship for an online footwear retailer. That internship gave him an introduction to e-commerce, search engine optimization, pay-per-click management, and affiliate marketing. After the internship was over, Nick decided to put his newly acquired skills to use by starting his own affiliate marketing business.

After graduation, Nick travelled to Costa Rica to participate in a Habitat for Humanity building project. While in Costa Rica, Nick's affiliate marketing business continued to generate revenue. Although the revenue wasn't significant, it gave Nick a taste of what it's like to earn passive income online.

After returning home from his trip, Nick got a full-time job for Ford Motor Company in the

Washington DC area. With his evenings and weekends free, Nick was determined to turn his part-time affiliate marketing business into something bigger. He sold his investment property for a healthy profit, and used some of the money to create his own website called *Shoes 'R Us* - a website that helped connect online shoe shoppers with the best deals from online retailers, earning an affiliate commission from the referral.

Nick's business was definitely not an overnight success. It took him 3 years of working evenings and weekends, but eventually his business grew to the point where keeping his job no longer made sense. That's when Nick left his job to "turn his side hustle into his main hustle" and become a full-time entrepreneur.

In 2009 Nick started blogging mostly because it seemed like a fun and creative way for him to share his ideas and experiences. That blog later evolved into what is now known as *Side Hustle Nation*, a blog and podcast dedicated to helping people learn how to turn their side hustles into successful businesses.

Nick has also published several books on Amazon, created an online course which is sold on Udemy, and helped many individuals start and grow successful businesses by offering coaching and consulting services. He is also the founder www.BusinessBookEditors.com, a freelance service specializing in proofreading and editing non-fiction business books.

To listen to my interview with Nick visit
www.chattingwithchampions.com/059

STRATEGY #5: COACHING & CONSULTING

Introduction to Coaching & Consulting

If you have a passion for helping others, coaching or consulting may be an attractive strategy for you. It is a way for you to share the wisdom and expertise you have in a specific area with someone who wants your help.

Logistically, working as a coach or consultant is very similar to working as a freelancer, but there are some distinctions. A freelancer is hired to do a specific *task*. A coach or consultant is hired to provide professional *advice*. A freelancer handles the *execution*. A coach or consultant helps create a *strategy*, and the execution of that strategy becomes their client's responsibility.

The difference between a coach and a consultant:

A consultant is someone whose relationship with their client lasts for the duration of a specific project. They are typically hired by the client to help solve a specific *problem* or achieve a specific *result*. Once that problem is solved (or that result is achieved), their services are no longer required. There are many different types of consultants including management consultants, leadership consultants, debt consultants, social media consultants, and marketing consultants, just to name a few.

A coach is someone who is hired by the client to help them experience a *transformation* of some kind. That transformation could apply to any area of their life including their relationships, health, finances, career, business, parenting, productivity, and more. Some individuals will hire multiple coaches at the same time, each for a different purpose. The relationship between a coach and their client can last as little as a few months, up to several years or longer.

Benefits of Coaching & Consulting

Here are some of the benefits of running a coaching or consulting business:

1. **Coaching and consulting is one of the fastest growing industries in the world**

The amount of information that is available to each and everyone one of us is overwhelming. This is precisely why so many individuals, and organizations, are choosing to hire coaches and consultants to help them devise a strategy to achieve their goals that is unique to their specific circumstances.

Advances in technology have transformed the way many of us do business. We are operating in a global marketplace, competing for opportunities, talent, and resources from all over the world. New industries are created almost overnight, and existing industries must find ways to adapt to a dynamic marketplace, or they will inevitably face extinction. Millions of people are unsure whether their roles will even exist in a few years.

Despite these conditions, coaching and consulting is one industry that continues to experience significant and consistent growth every year. According to Forbes, consulting is a $100 billion per year industry. The US Bureau of Labor Statistics predicts that consulting will grow by 83% by 2018. Now is one of the best times in history to profit from sharing your advice.

2. Low costs, high net profits

One of the most attractive benefits of coaching and consulting are the profit margins. The costs to run a coaching or consulting business are incredibly low. You can essentially run your entire business from a computer. Apart from an internet connection, website hosting fees, and an online calendar or scheduling software, the fixed costs required to maintain your business are inconsequential.

Working with additional clients does not cost you more money, it only costs you more time. Your fixed costs remain the same whether you work with 1 client or 10, hence the high net profits. Most coaches or consultants conduct their calls using Skype, which is free when the person you're calling also uses Skype. If you decide to host webinars, do group coaching calls, or use screen recording software, you may incur some additional costs, but they will be minimal.

3. You are not paid for your time

As a coach or consultant, you must trade your time in order to work with your client. But your client isn't paying you for your time, what they are really paying you for is the *value of the result* you help them achieve. Therefore, you can command fees that are in direct proportion to the value of that result, not the amount of time it takes you to help them achieve it. Depending on your specific industry and your positioning/authority in that industry, coaching or consulting can be very lucrative.

Let's pretend you're a marketing consultant who specializes in helping service-based businesses increase their revenue by utilizing various online marketing strategies. One of your clients currently generates $500,000 per year in annual revenue. You help them to create a strategy that will increase their annual revenue by 20% (the equivalent of $100,000) in the next 12 months. You charge them a consulting fee of $10,000.

This client happens to be local, so you have a face-to-face meeting to learn about their business before you develop the strategy. After agreeing to work together, you proceed to guide them through the implementation of your strategy via weekly phone calls for a period of 1 month. You track their results for the subsequent 5 months, communicating mostly through email, to ensure they remain on track and to revise the strategy if necessary. Between the meetings, phone calls, and email communication, you spend approximately 20 hours working with this client.

What is your time worth in this scenario? Your $10,000 fee divided by 20 hours equals $500 per hour. That number may seem high to some people, but remember, the client is not paying you for your time. They are paying you for the value of the result you helped them achieve. A $10,000 investment on their part to create an additional $100,000 in revenue in the next 12 months is good value.

4. Freedom, flexibility, and fulfillment

Coaching or consulting has many of the same benefits as freelancing. You can work from anywhere in the world as long as you have an internet connection. You can conduct your calls during whatever days and times work best for you and your clients. You can charge whatever fee is appropriate based on the value of the result you are able to help your clients achieve. You can choose who you work with and what services you provide to them.

Most importantly, you can experience fulfillment knowing that you are making a difference in your clients' lives. You get to be a part of helping them create the personal and professional transformations that they didn't have the knowledge, skills, or motivation to accomplish on their own. You get to see them succeed, and know that you played a part in their success. And in many cases, you get to develop meaningful friendships with your clients that last beyond the duration of your professional relationship with them.

CASE STUDY: GABRIEL PADVA

After graduating from university with a Bachelor of Commerce degree, Gabriel Padva worked as an inside sales and strategic partnership manager for a software company. It was a good job, one that helped Gabriel learn many valuable skills, including sales. But Gabriel dreamed of owning his own business, and so after just one year, he left his job to start his first company.

In 2006, Gabriel co-founded *Evolve Investment Group*, a real estate investment company that over a period of just 2 years was able to acquire over $15 million in assets in Canada's fastest growing economic regions. Part of that success was due to the incredibly effective inside sales system that Gabriel had developed for the company. That system enabled their sales team to go from having casual meetings over coffee with potential clients a few times per week (something that most of Gabriel's competitors were doing) to filling their calendar with pre-qualified sales appointments.

After a few years of working as the CEO for the real estate company, several of Gabriel's industry peers had taken notice of his company's success and were curious to learn about the sales system he had developed for the company. That's when he saw an opportunity to introduce his system to others. At the end of 2009, Gabriel decided to sell the real estate company and start his own consulting business: *30,000 FT Strategies*.

In order to gain experience and collect some testimonials from satisfied clients, Gabriel did some pro-bono work for non-profits. He also worked with some of his personal friends at a discounted rate. This allowed Gabriel to test and refine his systems and materials before charging a premium for his consulting services.

To date, Gabriel has successfully assisted over 50 companies to increase their revenue and improve their sales systems. By utilizing various software and communication tools, Gabriel has designed his consulting business so that he can run it from virtually anywhere in the world as long as he has an internet connection. Because he only works with a few select clients at any given time, he has the freedom to travel, be with his family, and generally do what he wants with his time, while still generating a multiple six-figure annual income.

To listen to my interview with Gabriel, visit
www.chattingwithchampions.com/051

Getting Started as a Coach or Consultant

1. Consider your experiences and expertise

Depending on the industry, you may be required to obtain certain credentials before you can charge someone for your services. However, the *most important* requirement is that you know how to help someone create the specific *outcome* that they are paying you to help them create. With or without credentials, if you can't help someone get the outcome they want, you won't last long.

Consider all of your past experiences and areas of expertise. Ask yourself the following questions:

- *What challenges have you overcome that you could help someone else with?*
- *What result have you achieved that you could help someone else achieve?*
- *What skills have you acquired that you could teach to someone else?*
- *What pain or frustration have you experienced but learned how to overcome?*
- *What mistakes have you made that you could help someone else avoid?*

The answers to these questions will help you determine what value you can extract from your personal and professional experiences, and that can be used to help someone else.

2. Identify your customer avatar

Once you've identified the areas in which you are able to help someone, the next step is to identify who is most likely going to want your help. A mistake many aspiring coaches and consultants make is assuming they can help everyone. A relationship coach, for example, could assume that *everybody* wants to have better relationships. But from a marketing perspective, trying to attract everybody is a big mistake. You need to get specific.

Your customer avatar is essentially a representation of your ideal client. It's the specific combination of demographics and psychographics that make them most suitable for you and you most suitable for them. *What is their age, gender, education level, profession, income? What are their habits, beliefs, fears, pains, frustrations, goals, aspirations?* The more you know about your ideal client, the more equipped you will be to influence them to take action and create change.

Here is an example of a vague customer avatar:

A woman who wants to start her own business.

Here is an example of a specific customer avatar:

> *A 35-45 year old single mother who works as an executive for a medium sized business earning approximately $80,000 per year. She works an average of 60 hours per week including her commute, and desperately wants to start her own business so she can have more control of her schedule and spend more time with her children. She has been dreaming of starting an online business for several years, but she doesn't know where to start. She needs someone to show her how to build her business in the little spare time she has, so she can eventually quit her job and work from home full time.*

3. Position yourself as the person who can help them

As you go through the exercise of identifying your customer avatar, you will develop a thorough understanding of the specific challenges they are facing, and more importantly, the *result* they want to create. Armed with that knowledge, your next step is to position yourself as the person who is able to help them get that result.

The first step to positioning yourself as the person who can help them is to write your *Unique Value Proposition* (UVP). Your UVP is essentially your answer to the inevitable question *"what do you do?"* (just so you know, when someone asks you this, what they are really asking is *what can you help them with?*). A strong UVP positions you as the go-to person in your niche. To create your UVP, answer the following 3 questions:

1. What type of person do you help?
2. What is the problem they are facing?
3. What is the result they want?

Now take the answers to each those questions and put them in a single sentence. Using the customer avatar from the previous step as an example, your UVP might sound something like this:

"I show female executives how to build an online business in their spare time, so they can quit their job, work from home and spend more time with their family."

Write several different versions of your UVP until you find one that feels right and is the most compelling to your customer avatar. Once you've got it, use it in your marketing. Include it on your website, in your bio, on your business cards, etc. Once you do, you will literally start to attract your customer avatar, because when they see that message, they will feel as if you are speaking to them directly.

4. Design your offer

Once you know who your customer avatar is and what result they want to create, it is time to create your offer. Your offer is essentially the step-by-step process you will guide each client through to help them get from where they are to where they want to be. This will be tailored to each client's unique circumstances and desired outcomes, but having a pre-determined framework will bring structure to your coaching or consulting process.

Questions to consider:

- *How will you communicate with your client? In person? Skype? Email?*
- *How often will you communicate? Weekly? Bi-weekly? Monthly?*
- *Will you work 1-on-1 or with groups?*
- *How long will the relationship last? 3 months? 6 months? 12 months?*
- *How much will you charge them?*
- *How will you charge them? Upfront? In instalments?*

As you answer these questions you should consider the format that would be most suitable for your client, and that also makes the most sense for your business and lifestyle goals.

How To Get Your First Client

1. Offer a free consultation

A coaching or consulting relationship begins with a free consultation. To start booking free consultations, add an application page to your website and begin directing potential clients to that page. Make it a requirement for someone to complete an application form in order to schedule their free consultation with you. A detailed form helps pre-qualify applicants. The people who actually take the time to complete the form are the most serious. The ones who don't are probably people you wouldn't want to work with anyway.

Your application form should include questions about their current business or profession, the goals or results they want to accomplish, the challenges they are facing that are preventing them achieving those results on their own, why they want your help, etc. The more detailed the application form, the better. Their responses to these questions will help you prepare for your initial call with them.

2. Conduct the first call

The purpose of a free consultation is *not* to convert someone into a client. It is a discovery call, not a sales call. Your objective is to *discover* where they are now, where they want to be, and what they need to help them get there. Most of the call will consist of you asking them the specific questions that will give you the information you need to determine whether or not you will be able to help them get the result they want, and if so, how you will do it.

Once you obtain the information you need, tell them you are going to prepare some specific recommendations for them, which you will present during your next call with them. Then schedule a follow up call. Remind them that you will not be charging them for this second call and there is no obligation on their part.

3. Come up with a strategy and create a proposal

Review your notes from the initial call, and start preparing your recommended strategy for helping them achieve the result they told you they want. In most cases it is appropriate to create a formal proposal. A proposal outlines the specific outcome they want to achieve, the strategy to be implemented, the logistics of working together (length of relationship, communication method and frequency, payment terms, etc.)

Depending on the scope of the proposed agreement/project, it may be best to send the prospective client a copy of this proposal prior to your follow-up call with them. This will give them some time to review it so that your follow-up call with them can be focused on answering any questions or concerns that they may have about your proposal.

4. Conduct a follow-up call

The purpose of this call is to present your strategy or recommendations to your prospective client. Start with a quick review of what was discussed during the first call. Clarify your understanding of their current circumstances, the challenges they are facing, and the desired result they need help to achieve. This helps to build trust, and shows them that you care enough to really understand their needs.

Once you've done that, proceed to share your recommendations. The key here is to provide as much value as possible before asking for their business. When your *free advice* adds significant value to them, they can't help but think that paying you for an ongoing relationship would be a wise investment.

5. Get an agreement

Your recommendations are essentially the road map your prospective client will need to travel in order to get the outcome they want. Once you've painted that picture, the next step is to ask them if they want you to help make that happen for them.

Remember, coaching and consulting is about providing the strategy. The execution of that strategy is your client's responsibility. They are paying you to guide them as they execute. Tell them what that will look like. Walk them through the logistics of working with you, your pricing, terms and conditions. If they're ready to work with you, get an agreement in writing and get started!

CASE STUDY: JESSE KRIEGER

From an early age, Jesse Krieger dreamed of becoming a rock star. When he was 18 years old he left his hometown of San Francisco to attend the Los Angeles Music Academy. From there, he headed to Europe where he played guitar in pubs and bars for a year before moving to Nashville, Tennessee to attend the School of Audio Engineering. It was in Nashville that he met his band mate and first business partner, and together they began writing songs and producing music.

As the band built a name for itself, Jesse and his partner reached a fork in the road. They could either try to get a deal with a major record label, or take the road less travelled and start their own label. After much debate, they agreed to start their own label with the understanding that Jesse would run the business side of things. And so at age 21, Jesse's journey down the road of entrepreneurship had begun.

The transition from musician to entrepreneur opened up a whole new world for Jesse. Forced to learn about business plans, raising money, hiring and managing staff as well as all the other things that are required to start a record label, Jesse developed a fascination for entrepreneurship and business in general.

After spending nearly 10 years in the music industry, Jesse decided to move back to San Francisco. From there, he launched *Krieger Consulting Group* and started helping other business owners grow their companies. Starting with the connections he made in the music industry, he quickly branched out and starting working with clients in a variety of industries.

Over the next few years Jesse became involved in several different businesses – from investment banking, to facilitating dating coaching seminars around the world, to co-founding a USB Superstore with operations in China. Before his 30th birthday, Jesse started over five companies and sold the last two. He's also lived in, worked in, and traveled to more than thirty countries, learning to speak a total of 3 languages along the way.

In 2014, wanting to share his experiences and the important lessons he's learned as an entrepreneur, Jesse wrote a book called *Lifestyle Entrepreneur*. Today, as the founder of *Lifestyle Entrepreneurs Academy*, Jesse teaches other entrepreneurs how to live their dreams and run their business from anywhere in the world through his coaching and online training programs.

To listen to my interview with Jesse visit **www.chattingwithchampions.com/046**

SUCCESS PRINCIPLES OF LIFESTYLE ENTREPRENEURS

As I mentioned in the preface of this book, the one thing I learned several years ago is that the specific strategy you choose to build your business is not nearly as important as the underlying principles you will need to abide by in order to become successful. If you learn a strategy but you don't understand the underlying principles that are foundational to long-term success, you will most likely experience failure.

In this section of the book, I'll be introducing you to 7 specific principles that lifestyle entrepreneurs abide by and that enable their success regardless of which strategies they use to make money in their business. Strategies can change all the time, but principles are timeless, and they apply to *all* industries and niches. Learning and abiding by these principles will help ensure you have the highest chances of succeeding as you implement the strategies that were outlined in the previous section.

PRINCIPLE #1: Think Like An Entrepreneur

Having the right mindset is the single most important principle of succeeding as an entrepreneur. Compared to the general population, a very small percentage of people are able to pay for their desired lifestyle from the profits of their own business. This is because it takes a very unique mindset to succeed in business. It takes an *entrepreneurial mindset.*

Most people work for someone else. They take whatever skills they have and put those skills to use for an employer. Whether they are paid by the hour for those skills or they receive a salary, the underlying fact is that they are paid for their time. In order to make money, they must trade their time. When they trade their time, they get paid. It's a simple concept of which everyone is familiar with. Consequently, most employees adopt a mindset towards making money that is very linear. *"If I make $20 per hour and I work 40 hours per week, I will make $800 per week." "If my annual salary is $60,000 and I work an average of 50 hours per week, my time is worth approximately $24 per hour."*

If you tell an employee that your business did $1,000 in sales last night while you were sleeping you might see a look of confusion on their face. To someone with an employee mindset, making money without trading your time conflicts with their belief system about how money is made. A linear mindset towards making money will not serve you as an entrepreneur. If you have that mindset, get rid of it.

Entrepreneurs are not paid for their time

Entrepreneurs are not paid for their time; they are paid for the *value* they deliver to the marketplace. They are paid for their *results*. The catch is that *it can take a lot of time to learn how to get results*. But once you put that time in, you can create those results over and over again with little effort.

One of the reasons so many people quit before they succeed as an entrepreneur is because they expect immediate compensation for their time *before* they create results. They mistakenly believe that the marketplace should reward them for the *time* they've invested, and not for the *value* that they delivered to the marketplace. They approached business with an employee mindset, not the mindset of an entrepreneur.

There is no need to get emotional

If you've ever watched a game of poker or sat at the table, you know that the best players are also the best at concealing their emotions. Their facial expressions hardly change, hence the term "poker face". This makes it difficult for their opponents to assess the confidence (or lack of confidence) they have in their hands.

Approach building your business the same way you would approach a game of poker. Check your emotions at the door. If you place an ad and no one clicks on it, don't cry about it. Learn from it and change your ad. If you send an email to your list and it causes many people to unsubscribe, don't get frustrated. Learn from it and move on. Learn to view all results as *feedback*. Who cares if the feedback is good or bad - it's all valuable. When you do something wrong, the feedback you get teaches you a valuable lesson. When you do something right, you make money. Either way, you benefit.

PRINCIPLE #2: Serve A Hungry Market

Before you create a product or service (or market someone else's product or service) you must know exactly who that product is intended for. Marketing is about identifying the needs of a specific audience and then matching those needs with a product or service. Once you have identified your target audience you can begin positioning your product as the solution to their most pressing needs or frustrations.

Give your audience what they are hungry for

Imagine for a moment that there are two separate rooms, each containing 100 people. In the first room these 100 people were just served an exquisite dinner. The dinner was so exquisite that most of these people had a second plate. Very few people even have room for dessert. In the second room there are 100 who have been locked in that room for 3 days and given nothing but water to drink. They are starving. They would eat anything that they could get their hands on. You have 100 sandwiches with a retail value of $10 each. Which room do you approach?

Offering your sandwiches to the first room is nonsensical. Not only would very few people in that first room want to buy a sandwich from you, but you might even have to offer a discount just to entice them to do so. You'd be lucky to sell a dozen sandwiches, even at half price.

The wiser choice would be to offer your sandwiches to the room full of 100 starving people. These people are starving for what you're offering, and price is probably not even a concern of theirs. Each person in that room would likely be willing to pay $20, $30, heck maybe even $50 for a single sandwich. You wouldn't have any trouble selling all 100 sandwiches, even if you charge a premium.

So why is it nonsensical to sell your sandwiches to the first room and wise to sell them to the second room? Because if you sell to the second room you are presenting your product to an audience that is starving for that product. You solved their problem (hunger), and they *happily paid you* for doing so. The people in the first room already solved that problem, so your product is of no use to them. This is where the term *hungry market* comes from.

Successful entrepreneurs present their product or service to an audience that is *hungry* for that product. If your product isn't selling, it may simply be because you're presenting it to the wrong audience. To succeed as an entrepreneur, find a hungry market and give them what they want.

Talk to your audience

To find out what your audience is "hungry" for, *ask them*. Talk to your existing customers, prospects, and website visitors on a regular basis. Ask them about the challenges they are facing, the information they need, the results they want, and why. When you truly understand the needs of your audience, you will be better positioned to create and/or recommend products and services that provide them with the solution they are hungry for.

PRINCIPLE #3: Your List = Leverage

Regardless of which niche you build your business in or which strategy you use, an email list of existing and potential customers is the most valuable asset your business can have. Having a list of people who know who you are, who have expressed interest in your products or services, and who have given you permission to communicate with them becomes your greatest source of recurring revenue. Building your email list is therefore one of the single most profitable activities you can do for your business.

The reason why having a list is so important is because very few people will buy from you the first time they visit your website or see your offer. And unless you obtain their email address, you have no way to follow up with them. You need to give them a reason to subscribe to your email list so you can continue to communicate with them after they've left your website (or listened to your podcast, or read your book, etc.).

Size doesn't always matter

Although the size of your list is important, it is not as important as the *relationship* you build with your list. A list of 100 satisfied and loyal customers is worth much more to you than a list of 1,000 people with whom you have no credibility and who have never bought from you before.

In order to build a great relationship with your list you must continuously provide your subscribers with *value*. If all you do is solicit them with your offers, it won't be long before they unsubscribe from your list. You need to consistently provide them with valuable information that is going to help them in order to earn their trust. Once that trust is established, you will experience much better results when you decide to promote a product or service to your list.

To start building your list of email subscribers, you will need to use email marketing software. Aweber is a great option for this. They only charge $1 for the first month, and after that, their monthly fee increases in proportion to the size of your list. Once your account is set up, follow these steps:

1. Write your first auto-responder

An auto-responder is an email that will be sent automatically to each new subscriber to your list. When someone joins your list, Aweber will send them a confirmation email. Once they confirm that they would like to receive your emails, they will be sent the first auto-responder. In this first email, thank them for subscribing and tell them what they can expect in your future emails.

2. Create an opt-in form

An opt-in form is the form you put on your website that collects someone's email. You can create an opt-in form using Aweber, or you can install a separate plugin on your website to create one. Most plugins have the ability to connect with your Aweber account.

3. Create a lead magnet

A lead magnet is something that you offer to someone in exchange for joining your email list. It is called a lead magnet because it "attracts" people to your email list. It can be a free book, a PDF guide, a video training series, etc. Include the title and/or image of your lead magnet in your opt-in form. For example: "Free guide reveals _____. Enter your email in the form below to get instant access!" Include a link to download whatever was offered in the first email that gets sent to new subscribers.

4. Write a follow-up sequence

A follow-up sequence is a series of follow-up emails that are sent to each subscriber according to a predetermined schedule. Remember, the purpose of having an email list is to build a relationship with your list by providing them with valuable information over time. Fortunately, this can be automated.

For example, if you have 10 tips to share on a specific topic, you can write 10 separate emails to share those tips. If you schedule each email to be sent one week after the previous, every new subscriber will automatically receive 1 tip per week for a period of 10 weeks.

CASE STUDY: XAN BARKSDALE

After playing minor league baseball with the Atlanta Braves for 3 years, Xan Barksdale started working as a coach at the University of Louisville, where he stayed for 5 years before becoming a coach at East Tennesse State University. While working as a coach, Xan decided to take his knowledge and passion for baseball, and start building his own online business.

Working in his spare time, Xan created his first product - a thumb protector for baseball catchers, which he appropriately called the *Catcher's Thumb*. He set up a website at www.catching-101.com and in an effort to spread awareness of his product, he started creating training videos which he published on YouTube. His videos linked to his website, so as the amount of views his videos received increased, so did his product sales.

Xan soon realized that due to the seasonal nature of his business, he would experience a spike in sales during baseball season followed by a decline in sales for the rest of the year. That's when he decided to explore other types of products so that he could create a more consistent income online.

Since 2008, Xan has produced training DVDs, developed software, iPhone applications as well as other physical products related to baseball. He's also written several books including *Catching-101*, *Big League Nutrition* and *Strength Training For Youth Athletes*. The combined revenue from all of these products now exceeds $100,000 annually.

To listen to my interview with Xan visit
www.chattingwithchampions.com/040

PRINCIPLE #4: Congruency

As an entrepreneur, you need to be congruent in your marketing. Being congruent means that all of the different tools you use to promote your business (your ads, your websites, your emails, your logos, your social media posts, etc.) all communicate the same message.

If you want people to buy from you, you need to make them feel like they came to the right place when they find you online. Marketing is all about getting the right message in front of the right audience. If your underlying message is unclear or constantly changing, you will repel potential customers from buying from you. When your message is congruent across all platforms, that congruency reinforces your brand.

Think about a person who keeps changing careers. First they're a financial advisor. The next day they're a real estate agent. Then they're a personal trainer. And then they become a life coach. Would you do business with them? Not likely. Successful entrepreneurs know who they are, what they stand for, and how they can help others, and they spend *years* reinforcing that brand in every single piece of communication with their audience. *Their marketing is congruent.*

Congruency in your sales funnel

Once you know what your target audience wants and what message they respond to best, you must use that message consistently throughout all your marketing.

The process that attracts your target audience, guides them to your offer, and converts them into a customer is called a sales funnel. A common sales funnel begins with an ad that is placed online. If your ad contains the right message and is displayed in front of the right audience, it will get clicked on. When someone clicks on it they will typically be directed to a sales page (often a video presentation or a written presentation for a product or service). After the presentation they will be given the option to buy. After they buy they may be upsold on related products before they receive a thank you message and a confirmation of their purchase.

If you have no congruence in your sales funnel (ie. your core message or promise keeps changing) you will likely confuse your prospect. Not having congruence also makes you look very unprofessional. Always make sure that each step in your sales funnel is congruent with the other steps.

Congruency in your behavior

The second aspect of congruency relates to your behavior. If you are in the business of telling people what to do, make sure you do those things too. Lead by example. Have integrity. Don't sell a program that tells people to run 3 times per week if you don't even do that yourself. Set the example for your audience. *People will watch what you do more than they listen to what you say anyway.*

PRINCIPLE #5: Focus On Income Generating Activities

One of the greatest benefits of building a lifestyle business is that, if you do it properly, you can generate enough income to replace your need to work for someone else. You get to be your own boss. The freedom that comes from working for yourself and generating enough income to pay for your desired lifestyle is unmatched. However, there is one big downfall to being your own boss: *you are your own boss*. Allow me to explain...

When you work for someone else it's easy to work hard and be productive with your day. It's easy because if you're not productive with your time, you know you'll soon be fired. But when you are your own boss, you can't exactly fire yourself. When there are no immediate consequences for being unproductive, it is much easier to waste time on unproductive activities. Most people do not succeed when they work for themselves because they are their own worst enemy. They do not have the discipline to focus their time or energy on activities that have the biggest impact on their bottom line.

Your business is not a hobby

Treat your business like you would any other job. *Do not treat it like a hobby.* Even if you are currently employed, you must set aside specific blocks of time throughout your week to devote exclusively to growing your business. If you will be working from home, you should designate a room in your house exclusively for working on your business. It is important that you have an environment to work in that is conducive to success and that allows you to focus. A home office is ideal. The living room where you spouse or kids spend time watching television is not. If you don't have the discipline to treat your business like a job, it won't be a business – it will be a hobby. Hobbies don't make money. They *cost* money.

Successful entrepreneurs constantly asks themselves *"What am I doing to grow my business?"* They are always doing what is the most productive thing to do at any given moment. They understand that there is a difference between being busy and being productive. Being busy means you are occupied with lots of activities and it feels like you're getting lots done. Being productive means you are *focused on a single activity* that yields the greatest return on your time invested. Being busy means *doing things right*. Being productive means *doing the right things.*

Focus on income producing activities

The Pareto Principle (also called the 80/20 Rule) states that 80% of results come from 20% of activities. In business, we call the 20% the *income producing activities*. These are the activities that, when performed, generate approximately 80% of the income. To be an effective entrepreneur, especially if you intend to build your business part-time, you need to focus the majority of your time on income producing activities. All the other activities that must be done but that do not have a direct correlation to your income should be delegated to someone else, or done *after* your income producing activities for the day are complete.

Examples of income producing activities:

- Promoting an offer to your list of subscribers
- Hosting a webinar with potential customers
- Lead generation (ie. *placing an ad online*)
- Talking 1-on-1 to a prospect (ie. *selling*)
- Creating a new product

Examples of non-income producing activities:

- Customer service
- Watching sales videos, info-products, training, etc.
- Book keeping
- Responding to unnecessary emails

- Graphic design
- Scrolling through your news feed on social media
- Editing/formatting

Successful entrepreneurs know how to protect their time. They deliberately spend the majority of their time on activities that yield the greatest return. It all boils down to simple math. If your goal is to generate $100,000 online in the next 12 months, and you are prepared to commit 500 hours to make that happen, then your time must be spent on activities that are worth at least $200 per hour to your business ($100,000 divided by 500 hours equals $200). Activities that are worth less than must be delegated. You cannot expect to earn $100,000 in the next 12 months if you spend your time on activities that can be delegated for $15 per hour.

PRINCIPLE #6: Automation & Outsourcing

This principle is closely related to the previous one. In order to be able to focus your time the activities that have the biggest impact on your business and that are aligned with your passions and strengths, you need to have systems or hire other people to handle certain activities for you. You most definitely do not want to do everything yourself.

Creating systems, automating processes, and outsourcing activities are critical steps required for creating the freedom that so many entrepreneurs crave. This may sound strange, but you want to remove yourself from your business as much as possible. You want to design your business so that it continues to provide value for others even when you're not actively working on it.

To begin removing yourself from your business as much as possible you'll need to identify all of the activities that need to get done on a regular basis but that you *should not* be doing yourself.

Take out a piece of paper and on it draw three columns. In the first column, list all of the activities required to keep your business running but that as an entrepreneur, you *should not* be doing yourself. In the second column, list the activities you *don't want* to do. In the third column, list the activities that you *can't* do (because you don't know how).

Completing this exercise will give you a very clear idea of the activities you should be outsourcing, leaving you with a small number of key activities that you enjoy doing, are good at doing, and should be doing yourself.

Even though the strategies discussed in the first section of this book all leverage technology and the internet, there are still numerous activities within each of those strategies that can be outsourced. If you run a blog, for example, you should probably be the one who writes the articles, but you should not be the one to edit, format, optimize for SEO, publish, or promote those articles. If you host a podcast, you should probably be the one conducting interviews or recording episodes for your show, but you should not be editing the episodes, uploading them to your media host, publishing them on your website, etc. These are all necessary activities, but they are not activities that *you* should be spending your time on.

Once you have a list of activities to outsource, the next step is to hire someone to take care of the activities for you.

Hire a virtual assistant

One step you can take to immediately reduce your workload and free up your time is to hire a virtual assistant. A virtual assistant (also called a VA) is someone who works for you remotely and provides administrative, technical, or creative assistance. It is not difficult to find highly qualified VAs to handle the activities that you should not be handling yourself.

You can hire a VA who lives in your own country, or you can hire someone in another country such as India or the Philippines where VAs are very common. You can eventually hire multiple VAs for various roles depending on the size of your business, but it is best to start with one and go from there. A VA works for you as an independent contractor. They are not your employee.

There are two ways you can hire a VA. You can do it yourself, or you can get in touch with an agency who will find one for you. If you choose to do it yourself, you'll need to create a job description, post an ad online (on Elance, Odesk, Guru, or even Craigslist), collect resumes, and do interviews using Skype until you find the one you want to hire. If you go through an agency, they will handle this process for you and match you with a suitable VA in exchange for a fee. Virtual

<u>Staff Finder</u> and <u>Mr. Outsource</u> are both great options for this.

CASE STUDY: ERLEND BAKKE

In 2007, Erlend Bakke was working as a branding consultant in London, England. It was his dream job; something he had worked towards attaining since university. But everything changed when his boss took him out for a drink one night and gave him the "this isn't working out" speech. And just like that, he was let go.

With no income and rent to pay he had to dig deep and ask himself the all-important question: "what should I really do with my life?" It turned out that building a company was a long forgotten childhood dream of his, so he decided to start his first company with a friend from university. After the business was up and running Erlend felt the business relationship was not working out so he decided to leave London and go back to Norway where he started a carbon copy of the same business.

Over the next few years he worked incredibly hard to make his business successful. But the hard work and long hours took a toll on Erlend. In 2010, while attending the National Achievers Congress in London, Erlend started to feel a pain in his chest. He left the conference early, and on the train ride home he had a panic attack and was taken to the hospital.

That experience served as a wake-up call for Erlend. He realized he needed to find a way to reduce the amount of time it took him to run his business so that he could live a more balanced lifestyle. He couldn't afford to hire more local employees at the time, so he decided to outsource some of his day-to-day business activities to people in the Philippines.

Not only did outsourcing enable Erlend to spend less time running his business, it also sparked the idea for an entirely new business. Erlend later founded *Mr. Outsource*, a company that helps busy entrepreneurs find and hire virtual assistants from the Philippines.

In 2013, Erlend published a book called *Outsourcing Mastery*, followed by his second book called *Never Work Again*. He then started training entrepreneurs how to start, run and own freedom businesses through his seminar *The Freedom Bootcamp*, his private membership website, and most recently, with his *Hardcore MBA Podcast*.

Today, Erlend runs three businesses, manages 25 employees in 2 countries, and generates a multiple six-figure annual income working an average of 10-20 hours per week. He spends most of his time between Oslo, London, San Francisco and Davao City in the Philippines.

To listen to my interview with Erlend, visit **www.chattingwithchampions.com/043**

PRINCIPLE #7: What Gets Measured Gets Improved

One thing all successful entrepreneurs pay close attention to is their conversion rates. A conversion rate is reflected in the percentage of people who take a specific action you want them to take. For example, if 100 people see your ad, and 10 of them click on it, then your ad has a conversion rate of 10%. If 500 people visit your sales page, and 75 of them buy your product, your sales page has a conversion rate of 15%.

Once you have an online business with a sales funnel that converts visitors into customers, making money becomes a science. *X* dollars spent on marketing yield *X* dollars in sales. All the guesswork behind making money is removed, because all you have to do is look at the conversation rates. Numbers don't lie. When you know your conversation rates, your success becomes a predictable, mathematical formula.

One of the most important conversion rates to keep track of is the conversion rate of your website traffic to your email opt-ins. *What percentage of people who visit your website join your email list?* Then, as you build your list, you'll want to know the conversion rate of your email subscribers to customers. *What percentage of your list eventually becomes a customer?*

Consider this example:

You market a variety of products online ranging from a few hundreds to a few thousand dollars each. You've been tracking these statistics for the past 12 months so you know exactly how much money you've made, how many people have subscribed to your email list, how many people have visited your website, etc.

In the past 12 months, your business generated $50,000 in sales from a total of 100 customers. You calculate that your average customer is therefore worth $500 ($50,000 divided by 100 customers).

Your list has 5,000 subscribers. This means your conversion rate from subscribers to customers is 2% (100 customers divided by 5,000 subscribers). This also means that every subscriber on your list is worth $10 ($50,000 divided by 5,000 subscribers) over a 12 month period.

You also know that over the last 12 months your website received 50,000 visitors. This means that your conversion rate from visitors to subscribers is 10% (5,000 subscribers divided by 50,000 visitors). This also means that each visitor to your website is worth $1 (50,000 visitors divided by $50,000). Keep in mind that this data only applies to a 12 month period, and does not consider the *lifetime value* of your customers.

Over the next 12 months, you want to double your sales from new customers to $100,000. This means you must acquire 200 new customers ($100,000 in sales divided by $500 each). *How can you make this happen?*

One way you can do this is to spend more money on marketing. If you can get 100,000 people to your website in the next 12 months, all else being equal, you should acquire 200 new customers. And since you know exactly how much a visitor to your website is worth (a visitor is worth $1), you know how much you can afford to spend to get a visitor based on the return on investment (ROI) that you want. If you want every dollar you spend on marketing to generate $2 in sales (100% ROI), then you can afford to spend $0.50 to get someone to your website.

Another option is to simply increase your conversion rates. If you can increase the conversion rate of website visitors to email subscribers, or email subscribers to customers, or both, then you can increase the amount of sales your business generates without having to increase the number of people that visit your website.

PUTTING IT ALL TOGETHER

In the introductory pages of this book I introduced you to the concept of *lifestyle entrepreneurship*. And while there is no "official" definition for the term, the one I shared with you seems to do it justice:

> *"A lifestyle entrepreneur is a business owner who prioritizes lifestyle benefits over profits. They organize and manage enterprises that can be fully or semi-automated, and are known for organizing their work and business activities around their lifestyle goals. Lifestyle entrepreneurs leverage other people and systems to run their business, are location-independent, and often work from home or while travelling."*

In the next section of the book, I introduced you to 5 specific strategies that you can use to make money doing something that you are passionate about: *blogging, podcasting, information marketing, freelancing, coaching and consulting.*

On their own, each of these strategies can be quite lucrative, but they also complement each other very well. As you learned from the case studies throughout this book, many lifestyle entrepreneurs have used several of these strategies simultaneously. That being said, it is best to start with just one single strategy. Commit to it until you make it work. Systematize and automate as much of it as possible before you introduce an additional strategy into your business.

In this second section of this book, I introduced you to 7 specific principles that lifestyle entrepreneurs abide by and that enable their success regardless of which strategies they use to make money in their business. These are equally as important as the strategies (if not more important), because if you learn a strategy but don't learn the underlying principles that enables someone to succeed, you are probably going to fail.

I truly hope that this book provided you with enough information to help you take the first steps towards building your own lifestyle business, and that the case studies served as a source of inspiration by showing you what can happen when you apply these strategies. Remember, information has very little value on its own. You must *take action* in order to reap tangible rewards.

I wish you all the best on your journey to become a *lifestyle entrepreneur*.

See you at the top,

Was this book helpful?

I do my best to write books that provide relevant and valuable information to my readers. I would love to hear what you thought of this book and how it measured against your expectations. All feedback is appreciated and used to improve current and future books.

You can contact me through my website
www.tylerbasu.com

To learn more about my other books visit
amazon.com/author/tylerbasu

To learn more about Lifestyle Business Magazine visit
www.lifestylebusinessmag.com

Printed in Great Britain
by Amazon